ALEXANDER THE GREAT
AN ILLUSTRATED MILITARY HISTORY

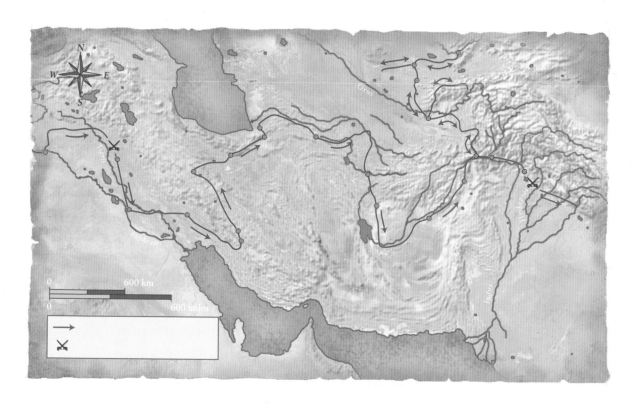

THE RISE OF MACEDONIA, THE BATTLES, CAMPAIGNS AND TACTICS OF ALEXANDER,
AND THE FALL OF HIS VAST EMPIRE AFTER HIS EARLY DEATH, DEPICTED IN 250 PICTURES

NIGEL RODGERS

southwater

This edition is published by Southwater, an imprint of Anness Publishing Ltd, Blaby Road, Wigston, Leicestershire LE18 4SE
info@anness.com

www.southwaterbooks.com; www.annesspublishing.com

Anness Publishing has a new picture agency outlet for images for publishing, promotions or advertising. Please visit our website www.practicalpictures.com for more information.

Publisher: Joanna Lorenz
Editor: Joy Wotton
Designer: Nigel Partridge
Illustrations: Vanessa Card, Anthony Duke, Peter Bull Art Studio
Production Controller: Christine Ni

ETHICAL TRADING POLICY
Because of our ongoing ecological investment programme, you, as our customer, can have the pleasure and reassurance of knowing that a tree is being cultivated on your behalf to naturally replace the materials used to make the book you are holding. For further information about this scheme, go to www.annesspublishing.com/trees

Previously published as part of a larger volume *The Rise & Fall of Ancient Greece*

PUBLISHER'S NOTE
Although the information in this book is believed to be accurate and true at the time of going to press, neither the authors nor the publisher can accept any legal responsibility or liability for any errors or omissions that may have been made nor for any inaccuracies nor for any loss, harm or injury that comes about from following information in this book.

CONTENTS

THE AGE OF ALEXANDER

The ancient Greeks were driven by two concepts: love of honour (*philotimaea*) and desire for *areté* (excellence, goodness, perfection, a term applicable to anything from athletics to philosophy). They were intensely competitive as individuals, striving 'always to be best'. These words of Homer, the greatest Greek poet, about his hero Achilles, inspired Alexander the Great when conquering the Persian Empire. But the pursuit of excellence was not restricted to individuals.

Alexander the Great remains one of the most dramatic figures in world history. He was indisputably a military genius, overthrowing the vast Persian Empire, but views about him remain divided. The Victorian historian Thomas Carlyle called him "Macedonia's madman". More recently he has been damned as a paranoid alcoholic, murdering all in his way, perhaps before being finally murdered himself. To many at the time – be they democrats such as Demosthenes, or inhabitants of cities that he erased, such as Thebes, Tyre or Persepolis – Alexander was purely destructive. But others have seen him as transcending Greek chauvinism, trying to create a global empire that united conquered and conquerors. To romantics he has always appealed. Alexander saw himself as a reincarnation of Achilles, the Homeric hero who preferred a glorious early death to long but obscure life. In this at least he succeeded: his name has passed into legend across Asia as well as Europe.

Alexander's dazzling successes were possible only because of the achievements of his father Philip, who created the best army yet seen. If a lesser general than his son, Philip was a better politician. Alexander's successors extended Greek power and culture across Asia, creating the civilization known as Hellenistic. Although endless wars wrecked many kingdoms,

Below: The Charioteer of Delphi, *dating from* c.470BC, *superbly exemplifies early classical sculpture. One of the very few bronze statues to survive, it was originally painted with lifelike colours.*

Above: Far from being always made of cold white marble, most Greek statues glowed with vivid colour, as shown in this kore, *a statue of a young girl of the 6th century* BC.

Greek culture continued to spread, finally influencing art in countries as distant as India and China. The last Hellenistic monarch to resist the rise of Rome was Cleopatra VII of Egypt, a queen of legendary glamour. But Alexander's final heir proved to be Rome itself.

MEN OF WAR

Throughout the Classical Age (*c*.500 –*c*.300BC) Greece was never unified into a large centrally controlled state. Instead, it remained divided into scores of fiercely independent city-states (as we translate the world *polis*, although 'citizen-state' might be more accurate).

This was partly due to geography. Lacking large river valleys or plains, Greece is divided by mountains into small valleys, which inherently encouraged such individualism. But the results made Greek civilization, as it developed focused on each *polis*, crucially different from all earlier civilizations. No one had really done politics (our word comes from *polis*) before the Greeks took to arguing and experimenting, at times violently, about the best forms of government.

A worse criticism of the Greeks would be their endless wars. Just enough city-states united to repel the Persian invasions of 490–478BC, but that unity proved unique. The Greeks reverted to fighting each other, often calling in outside powers – even Persia – to help. Such disunity led to their conquest, first by the Macedonians, then by the Romans. It was the dark side of the Greeks' pursuit of individual excellence or perfection.

THE PURSUIT OF PERFECTION

It was the Athenian people, the *demos*, who supported the building of the great temples of the Acropolis. The Athenian people attended the plays of the great dramatists Aeschylus, Sophocles and Euripides. The Athenian experience shows that democracy does not have to mean dumbing down to the lowest intellectual level: it can mean raising up a whole city to unprecedented cultural and political heights.

VIBRANT CLASSICISM

For many people ancient Greece can seem a cold, remote world of smooth marble statues and pristine white temples, lacking human interest. Such images mislead. Far from being cold and passionless, the Greeks burned and quivered with passions and desires – personal, political and intellectual – that often led to disaster, not perfection. Remember that Alexander saw himself as a reincarnation of Achilles, the principal hero of Homer's *Iliad*.

Few original Greek statues survive – a few in marble, even fewer bronzes. Too often we have only mediocre Roman copies of the great originals. We have lost even more Greek painting. What has survived, reveals that the Greeks pioneered a naturalistic art. The far more numerous extant vases, often magnificent artworks, tell us much about Greek daily life.

THE EXPANSION OF GREECE

Today the Greeks are confined to Greece proper and Cyprus. But in antiquity they spread – first all around the Mediterranean as far as Marseilles, and then across western and central Asia. This second expansion (336–323BC) occurred under Alexander the Great. A supreme military genius, Alexander overthrew the Persian Empire and founded many cities that helped to Hellenize (the Greeks called themselves Hellenes) western Asia. By 200BC, a traveller could go from southern France all the way to the borders of India speaking only Greek, at least in the cities.

This expanded Greek world fell in the end mostly to Rome, which by 30BC had conquered the Greeks, often with a greedy brutality. But the Romans, if lacking Greek brilliance, became superb preservers and transmitters of Greek culture (though not Greek democracy) across Western Europe. The resulting Graeco-Roman civilization is the bedrock of the modern world. The Greeks are not just ancient history buried in museums: their ideas, arguments, ambitions and culture have helped shape Western history since the Renaissance and still underly much of the modern world. To understand ourselves today, we need to look back to the Greeks.

Above: The influence of Greek art has persisted down the centuries. The front of the British Museum, London, built by Robert Smirke in 1823–46, consciously echoes Greek models.

Below: Among the most famous of Greeks, Alexander the Great of Macedonia (reigned 336–323BC) overthrew the Greeks' old enemy, the immense Persian empire, but also restricted their cities' cherished independence.

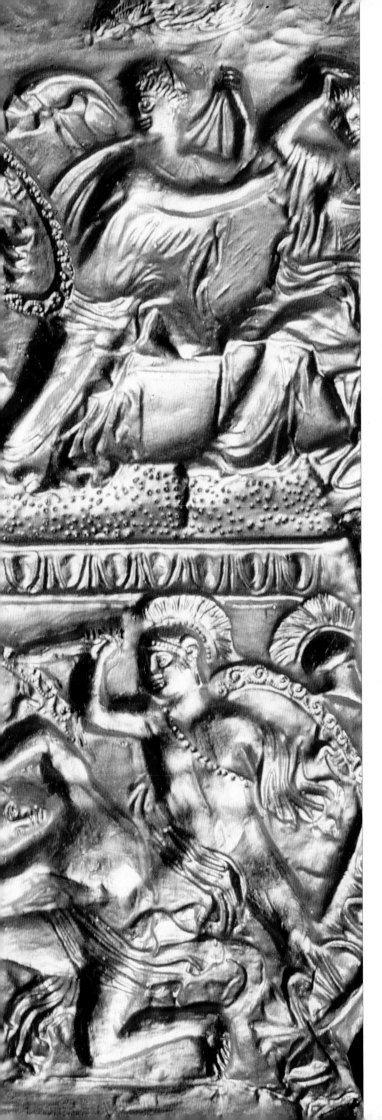

CHAPTER I

THE RISE OF MACEDONIA

359–336BC

Alexander's achievement appears so dazzling that his career has often eclipsed that of his father, Philip II. But without the patient state building of Philip, who started his reign in most unpromising circumstances and ended it as Greece's acknowledged leader, Macedonia would never have become the military powerhouse that it was by 336BC. In that year Alexander succeeded to the throne over his murdered father's body – a typical Macedonian scenario, some may have thought.

Several earlier monarchs had tried to unify this kingdom – which remained closer to the heroically chaotic world of Homer than a Greek *polis* – but their attempts had died with them, and their deaths had seldom been from natural causes. Although invaders and feuding nobles constantly threatened it, Macedonia was the largest, potentially wealthiest of Greek states. Endowed with fertile plains and wide pastures, it was occupied by a warlike people usually loyal to the throne if not always to the person occupying it. Yet Macedonia remained on the fringe of the Greek world until its meteoric rise under Philip II in the 350s BC. One of the most Machiavellian as well as energetic of rulers, Philip used bribes and promises as well as force to divide and conquer at home and abroad. After Philip's reign, Macedonia remained a major power in the Mediterranean world until the advent of Rome overwhelmed all the Greek states.

Left: Macedonia's new wealth and old martial energy are shown in this gold quiver from the royal tombs at Vergina.

EARLY OBSCURITY
c.480–359 BC

Above: Mt Olympus, the highest peak in Greece and mythical home of the gods, lay within the Macedonian kingdom. Greek-style games were held at Dion on its slopes.

North of Mt Olympus, the greatest mountain known to the Greeks, stretched a realm that few southern Greeks knew at all and one about which even fewer normally cared, even though Macedonia had long protected Greece proper from barbarians to the north.

It was a land-bound kingdom, the coastal cities such as Olynthus being mostly colonies of southern cities. Aegae, Macedonia's ancient inland capital, overlooked the rich Emathian plain near the sea. Macedonia itself could be roughly divided into two zones: the lowland area, where royal authority ran, and the highland zone to the north and west, which was mountainous and thickly forested. Here, in walled, isolated villages, Macedonians still lived lives that Homer might have recognized but that would have struck classical Greeks as uncouth. Often herdsmen or subsistence farmers, these 'Upper Macedonians', such as the Lyncestids, acknowledged only clan chieftains. Beyond these tribal communities lived real barbarians: Illyrians and Celts to the north and north-west and Thracians to the north-east,

waiting their chance to descend on the rich lowlands. Their invasions mattered much more to clans such as the Lyncestids or Orestids than to any distant king down on the coast, who could give them little protection against such attackers.

MACEDONIAN KINGS

The first notable Macedonian monarch was Alexander I (reigned 498–454 BC). His reign coincided with the great Persian invasion of 480 BC, in which he played an ambivalent role. He first accepted Persian overlordship in 491 BC, when the Persian general Mardonius led an army west along the Aegean's north coast. In 480 BC he involuntarily entertained King Xerxes himself – an expensive guest with his huge court and army – before accompanying the Persians south. But Alexander also sent ambiguously worded warnings to the Greeks. In spring 479 BC he acted as the Persian's go-between, trying to persuade Athens to change sides. This was an ignominious role, but other more typical Greek states, most notably Thebes, also 'medized' (supported Persia).

Despite this, Alexander I was called the 'Philhellene' and was credited with expanding the kingdom, his reign later being remembered as a golden age. He was succeeded by his son Perdiccas II (reigned 453–413 BC), who steered a delicately neutral path between the great powers of his age, Athens and Sparta. Brasidas, Sparta's greatest general in the Peloponnesian War, was invited north in 424 BC by Perdiccas (among other states) to counter Athenian power. However, king and Spartan soon quarrelled as their aims diverged.

Left: Pella was Macedonia's new capital, chosen by king Archelaus in 413 BC. In it the young Alexander III later was born and grew up, while Philip extended his power.

Above: Euripides, the Athenian playwright, was among the writers and artists invited to Macedonia by King Archelaus trying to Hellenize his rough kingdom.

A NEW CAPITAL

Under Archelaus (413–399BC), the capital was moved down to Pella near the coast, leaving Aegae as the ceremonial centre. A determined policy of modernization ensued. Archelaus half-tamed the warlords of upper Macedonia, uniting the two halves of his realm. The army was reorganized on professional lines and straight roads linking new forts were built, as Thucydides noted. The Athenian poet Agathon and playwright Euripides were welcomed to Pella – Euripides wrote his last tragedy *The Bacchae* there – while Zeuxis, the famous painter, lavishly decorated its new palace. Socrates, offered refuge in Macedonia when facing trial in Athens, quipped that none would go to Macedonia to see its king but all wanted to see his new palace. So Archelaus and his court were not barbarous. But after his death Macedonia entered a confused decade, with four kings in quick succession. Stability was restored by Amyntas III (393–369BC), father of Philip II and grandfather of Alexander, but Macedonia remained marginal to Greek politics.

Below: This stele of the young Xantos, from Pella, Macedonia's capital, was made c.400BC and is classically Hellenic in style.

MACEDONIANS: GREEKS OR BARBARIANS?

Alexander I was proud to be called *philhellene*, lover of things Greek, but this title was normally awarded to rulers who were definitely *not* Greek. Croesus of Lydia, the monarch overthrown by Persia in 546BC, was termed philhellene, as were some Asian rulers after Alexander. Many Greeks of the Classical Age thought that the Macedonians were barbarians, but the Boeotian poet Hesiod, writing c.700BC, considered them to be Greeks, speaking the same Aeolic dialect as the Boeotians. Two centuries later the Persians, encountering the Macedonians after conquering the Ionians, classed them as Greeks, albeit of a distinct hat-wearing type.

Certainly Macedonians were not savage like the Thracians and Illyrians further north. They may have had odd northern accents (they pronounced Philip as Bilip, for example) and no real *polis* or citizen-state, but the same was true of Aetolians in north-west Greece, and nobody disputed their right to attend the games reserved for Greeks. The Macedonian kings, the Temenids, claimed descent from the ubiquitous sons of Hercules, who, according to legend, had left Argos c.650BC to settle in Macedonia.

It helped Macedonia that Olympus, home of the gods, was within its boundaries and that the games held at Dion on its slopes were clearly Greek. Generally, southern Greeks accepted Macedonia's kings as true Hellenes but disdained their rough subjects, who still had to kill a wild boar or lion to be thought a proper man. After Alexander the Great, as Macedonia grew increasingly rich and sophisticated, such distinctions vanished.

PHILIP II: THE RISE TO POWER
359–334 BC

Above: A silver tetradrachm (4-drachmae coin) of 354 BC, when Philip II was starting to turn Macedonia into a great military power.

Below: The Roman-era amphitheatre at Philippi, the former city of Crenides refounded by Philip II as a military colony in 357 BC to guard his eastern frontier.

In 359 BC Perdiccas III of Macedonia, elder son of Amyntas III, was defeated and killed fighting Illyrian invaders on his western frontiers. At the same time savage Paeonians invaded from the north. These disasters eclipsed the modest yet real achievement of Perdiccas' reign: he had thwarted renewed Athenian attempts to regain Amphipolis (the crucial city on the River Strymon), briefly installing a Macedonian garrison there. Perdiccas left a son, Amyntas, aged two, but he also had a younger brother, Philip, aged only 24.

Philip had earlier been a hostage for three years in Thebes, where he had seen the training that at the time made Theban hoplites the best in the world. He reputedly also had an affair with Pelopidas, the much older general. On his brother's death, Philip took over the government, at first as regent for his infant nephew but soon becoming king himself. (Amyntas seems to have grown up weak-willed if not feeble-minded.)

Philip bought off the Paeonians – he knew the power of money – while defeating a pretender backed by the Athenians. Philip then released all the Athenian prisoners without ransom and openly renounced claims to Amphipolis, while secretly offering to swap it for Pydna, a free city in the Athenian Confederacy, so gaining Athens' support. He spent his first winter recruiting and training a new army. Early in 358 BC, with 10,000 infantry and 600 cavalry, he routed the Illyrians, killing 7,000 of them.

AN EXPANDING EMPIRE
In 357 BC Philip turned east and attacked Amphipolis, which appealed to Athens for help – in vain. Once Philip had captured Amphipolis, he kept it, outwitting the Athenians, who were preoccupied with revolts in their Confederacy and in Euboea. He also seized Crenides inland. He renamed it Philippi, making it a Macedonian military colony, the first of many. These moves secured his hold on Mt Pangaeus and its gold and silver mines.

He soon had the mines worked far more intensively than before to yield 1,000 talents a year – as much revenue as the Athenian Empire had enjoyed in its prime. "Money", Philip observed, "is the sinews of war". Soon after, he took Pydna and Potidaea, giving the latter to Olynthus. This, the most powerful Chalcidic city, had earlier sought Athenian support but now became his well-bribed ally, at least for a time. During his siege in 354 BC of Methone, another Athenian ally, Philip lost one eye, marring his good looks.

AN ASTUTE MARRIAGE
Angered by Philip's actions, Athens encouraged his northern neighbours (Thracians, Illyrians and Paeonians) to attack Macedonia, but he beat or bought

Above: Olympia, site of the quadrennial Panhellenic games where Philip's horses won a prize in 356BC, usefully boosting his Hellenic credentials.

them off, using his trusted general Parmenion. Philip also employed non-military means to secure his position. In 357BC he married Olympias, niece of the king of Epirus to his west. Whether romance or *realpolitik* guided his choice (the two reputedly caught each other's eye at a midnight mystery rite on Samothrace), it was an astute move, and Olympias quickly bore him a son, Alexander, in 356BC. News of the birth reached him at the same time as that of a victory for his horses in the Olympic Games, making him a happy king. But events at another site sacred to all Greece were to give him his biggest chance yet.

THESSALY, EPIRUS, THRACE

Since seizing Delphi and its treasuries in 356BC, tiny Phocis had become the most powerful state in Greece, its mercenary forces defeating all armies sent against it. These included Thebes' and, in 353BC, Philip's, but his troops in Thessaly were outnumbered. While Phocian power was built on a dwindling supply of stolen gold, Philip's was based on the rising power of Greece's largest state. Returning to Thessaly in 352BC with a larger army, Philip routed the Phocians at the Battle

of the Crocus Field. He was then acclaimed *tagus* (ruler) of Thessaly, displacing the tyrants of Pherae. This gave him Thessaly's superb cavalry and brought him to the borders of central Greece itself.

Here, however, he was thwarted. Eubolus, then dominating the Athenian Assembly, sent a force to hold the crucial pass at Thermopylae. Not wishing to fight what was still Greece's greatest city just yet, Philip retreated and turned his attentions north. In 351BC he expelled King Arybbas, his wife's uncle, from Epirus, establishing her suitably grateful brother in his place. He brought further western tribes into Macedonia, extending his power to the Adriatic.

On his other flank lay Thrace, mountainous and wild. Profiting from divisions between its quarrelling princes, Philip pushed into its interior, founding Philippolis, his second city, on the River Hebrus. His power now touched the Chersonese – that peninsula on the Dardanelles controlling Athens' essential grain supplies.

Above: A tetradrachm showing Philip on horseback wearing a kausia, *the traditional Macedonian broad-brimmed hat.*

Below: This mural depicts the Rape of Persephone. From a royal tomb at Vergina (ancient Aegae), it shows the latest Greek artistic styles being adopted in Macedonia.

A NEW ARMY AND A NEW STATE: THE RULE OF PHILIP II

*Above: The young Philip II,
a fine Roman copy of an
original Greek statue.*

*Below: Macedonia, lying
outside Greece proper, was
far bigger than any normal
Greek state but dangerously
exposed to northern invaders.
Once united, with its
frontiers secured and its
potential exploited, it
became the greatest power
in the Greek world.*

Philip created the most formidable
army Greece had yet seen, able to defeat
Greece and (under his son) conquer Asia.
It outclassed Sparta's professional armies,
invincible until defeated by Thebes in
371BC. Macedonia's army was huge (by
Greek standards), highly professional and
increasingly filled with national pride.
Philip had inherited a kingdom that was
oddly archaic if vigorous, looking back
to the Homeric age. He left it the
indisputable Greek superpower.

The Macedonian state consisted of two
parts: the king himself, who was war
leader, supreme judge, high priest and
government; and the Assembly of adult
male Macedonians, who also constituted
the army and acted as a crude court.
There were no elected magistrates or
Council as in a Greek *polis*. Nor was there
a dangerously powerful old hereditary
aristocracy, in lower Macedonia at least,
although family background still mattered
greatly. Philip promoted many new men,
whether they came from old Macedonia
or elsewhere.

*Above: This vase from the 4th century BC
depicts a rather fanciful battle scene.
While Philip's victories were still won by
his footsoldiers, cavalry was becoming
increasingly important.*

MACEDONIA'S MONARCHY

Unlike Persia, Macedonia was not an
absolute monarchy. Macedonians bared
their heads but did not bow before their
king, whom they addressed by name, not
as 'Majesty'. Any Macedonian could
appeal to Philip for judgement. Kings
ruled by hereditary right as members of
the Temenid dynasty. If there was more
than one claimant to the throne, who
succeeded depended on their luck and
skill in winning over generals and
courtiers. Their choice was then put to

TOUGHENED PROFESSIONALS

Demosthenes complained that Macedonian armies campaigned throughout winter, unlike those of Athens or Thebes, whose citizens had to return to their farms every autumn. Only the Spartans had done this in the past. Macedonians managed this because Philip, doubling his country's size, gave newly conquered lands as estates to his followers, with slaves to work them. This enabled many Macedonians to become full-time soldiers.

The slave-worked mines of Mt Pangaeus remained the basis of Philip's revenues, allowing him to mint gold coins, the first Greek to do so. Only Persia's Great King was richer. Yet Macedonia's army was even tougher than Sparta's. While most Greek armies allowed one servant per hoplite, Philip allowed only one attendant per ten hoplites and banned carriages for his officers. He forced his men to march 48km/30 miles or more a day, summer or winter, over rough tracks. They often had to carry 30 days of supplies on their backs, to keep baggage trains as small as possible.

Philip once reproved a soldier for washing with hot water, saying that only women who had given birth should be allowed such luxury. Women were anyway banned from camp. All this was highly effective, not least because Philip himself endured every hardship and danger, being repeatedly wounded. He had emulated Spartan discipline and toughness on a larger scale.

Above: Although horsemen in the ancient world had no stirrups to hold them in place, they could still fight effectively with both lance and sword, as this coin from Taranto of c.300BC shows.

the Assembly, who voiced approval by clashing their spears, not voting. So the monarchy had a broad popular base.

Once accepted, a strong king in practice had almost boundless power, while a weak one soon lost his throne and his life. A king had, above all, to lead the army. The core of this in 359BC was the Companions (*Hetairoi*), originally 600 upper-class Macedonian horsemen. Philip increased their numbers steadily until by 338BC this royal cavalry numbered 4,000. Philip invented the title 'Foot Companions' for six battalions comprising 9,000 heavy infantry and created the Shield Bearers, 3,000 crack foot guards who, on the battlefield, linked the cavalry and infantry. He reorganized the army by forming battalions more on a territorial or tribal basis than a clan one. By 338BC he could field about 30,000 infantry and 5,000 cavalry, besides garrisoning numerous forts across his empire. This was unprecedented power.

USE OF THE PHALANX

Philip's chief military development was the much-improved phalanx, now a bristling porcupine of spear-men. They carried longer spears than ordinary hoplites: sarissas up to 5m/15ft long. No one could hold such a spears in one hand, so shields became smaller, being slung on the left arm. The phalanx was often massed up to 60 men deep (Philip remembered Theban examples) and was geared for attack, its flanks being covered by other troops. Discipline was vital to maintain formation, but with experienced Macedonian pike-men the phalanx could deliver an unstoppable punch. Philip also hired archers from Crete and engineers such as Polyeidus of Thessaly, who developed siege engines and catapults.

CREATING A UNITED KINGDOM

To unite his kingdom, Philip transplanted populations, settling highlanders in his new cities such as Philippi. He forced upland barons to send their sons to become royal pages at Pella, where they learned soldiering, royal service and some Hellenic culture – and acted as hostages. Philip cemented his power by seven marriages, including one to an Illyrian princess and two to Thessalians. But his prime marriage long remained that to Olympias of Epirus, Alexander's mother.

Below: A view of Pella, the thriving Macedonian capital under Philip II and his successors, where Alexander grew up, with a fine mosaic pavement in the foreground.

CONQUEROR OF GREECE
349–336 BC

Above: Philip II was notably handsome until he lost an eye at Methone in 354BC.

Below: Philip's greatest victory came in 338BC at Chaeronea, when he gained control of Greece. This lion, erected later over the mass grave, honours the Theban dead.

In 349BC Philip attacked Olynthus, his former ally and leader of the Chalcidic League. He had an excuse – Olynthus had aided a Macedonian rebel – but Philip had long had his eye on this, the richest city in north Greece. Roused by Demosthenes' impassioned oratory, Athens finally sent the city help in the form of 2,000 men, but they were too few and too late: Philip captured Olynthus in 348BC, destroying it and enslaving its inhabitants. He then annexed the other Chalcidic cities, whose leaders he had often bribed beforehand (he was as good at bribery as he was at strategy). Stagira, which resisted, was destroyed. With his power further boosted, Philip turned south. Athens, exhausted by minor wars around the Aegean and recurrent problems in Euboea, badly needed peace, but she was to get it on unfavourable terms.

AMPHICTYONIC COUNCIL LEADER

In 347BC the Thebans, unable to repulse the Phocians still ravaging western Boeotia, appealed to Philip to become leader of the Amphictyonic Council theoretically controlling Delphi. This was the opening he had long wanted. Sending friendly letters to potential supporters in Athens, Philip invited Greek envoys to Pella, kept them waiting while he conquered more Thracian forts and then proposed peace on the terms of the status quo. During the extended diplomatic exchanges, he suddenly marched south, passing Thermopylae, where the Phocian commander Phalaecus surrendered in exchange for his liberty.

Philip then invited the Athenians to send envoys to another conference to deal with Phocian sacrilege, but Demosthenes persuaded them to ignore his offer. Philip, dominating the Amphictyonic Council, dealt with the Phocians quite lightly, fining them and breaking them up into villages, taking Phocis' seat on the Amphyctionic Council for Macedonia. That year he presided over the Pythian Games held at Delphi. He could now pass as a true Hellene; he also seemed a lesser evil to many small states than Sparta, still feared for its past misrule. At the Peace of Philocrates in 346BC Athens had to accept terms that gave her nothing important while Thebes, Philip's new ally, regained its hegemony over Boeotia. This rankled with the Athenians. For Philip, the peace brought vital recognition of his position in central Greece.

OPEN WAR

Philip did not sit on his laurels. He led his army north-west into wildest Illyria, reaching the Adriatic probably near modern Dubrovnik. Then he turned north-east to annex Thrace. During this campaign, in which he reached the Danube, he fell seriously ill and was also wounded again. Demosthenes, in his 'Philippics' speeches, mocked the "limping one-eyed monster so fond of danger that to increase his empire he has been wounded in every part of his body". But Philip's campaigns had a purpose. With troops on the Black Sea and Sea of Marmara, he could now threaten Athens' crucial grain supplies from the region. Meanwhile, his envoys poured gold into the pockets of potential friends across Greece. These included Aeschines, Demosthenes' chief opponent in Athens.

In 340BC Philip, returning from the Danube, attacked Selymbria and then Byzantium on the Bosphorus. He captured neither, mainly because he lacked ships to counter Persian and Athenian naval support, but late in 340BC he seized

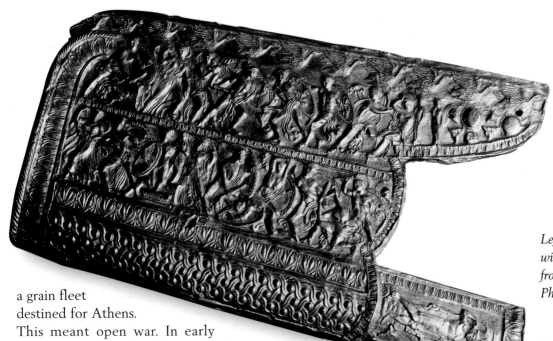

Left: Gold quiver decorated with scenes of soldiers fighting, from the probable tomb of Philip at Vergina.

a grain fleet destined for Athens.

This meant open war. In early 339BC Philip led his army swiftly down through Thessaly, bypassing Thermopylae into Phocis, where he seized the town of Elataea. His excuse was that further problems over Delphi required his assistance. In reality, Macedonia's main army now directly threatened Athens.

Demosthenes' finest hour had arrived. He had sensibly prepared for it by naval reforms, making the trierarchy, by which the richest citizens paid for triremes, more equitable. But Philip was a threat *on land*. Demosthenes now persuaded Athens to offer Thebes, its disliked neighbour but one with a powerful army, full alliance. Athenian concessions won Thebes over and Philip finally faced the two greatest powers in old Greece united. On 2 August 338BC the armies, which were roughly equal in size if not skills, met at Chaeronea.

BATTLE OF CHAERONEA

Philip placed the 18-year-old Prince Alexander on his left commanding the crack Companion cavalry opposite experienced Theban hoplites. He himself led the Footguards facing the Athenians. Philip advanced, attacked and suddenly seemed to flee. The Athenians pursued him recklessly, opening a great gap behind them. Through it charged Alexander to surround the Thebans. Philip then counter-attacked, soon routing Athens' citizen-soldiers. But the crack Theban Sacred Band, 150 pairs of homosexual lovers, fought to the last man. Athens lost over 1,000 dead with 2,000 taken prisoner. Chaeronea, a resounding triumph for Philip, was a disaster for Greek freedom.

Below: Byzantium (today Istanbul) shown in a 16th-century Ottoman map. Philip suffered one of his rare defeats when he besieged this city, vital to controlling grain supplies through the Bosphorus, in 340BC. But he still managed to seize a grain fleet destined for Athens.

PHILIP: TRIUMPH AND DEATH
338–336 BC

As undisputed victor, Philip could dictate the peace terms. Athens had to surrender the Chersonese (Dardanelles peninsula), becoming dependent on Macedonia's goodwill for the safety of its grain fleet. But in other ways, as even Demosthenes admitted, the peace was generous to her. She regained Oropus, long disputed with Thebes, and paid no indemnity. She also got back her prisoners without ransom, while young Prince Alexander ceremoniously returned the ashes of her dead soldiers. In return, the Athenians erected a statue to the Macedonian king. Philip's leniency to Athens was based on realism: Athens still had her long walls and large fleet, which would have made a direct attack very difficult. He also wanted her naval support for his anti-Persian crusade, while attacking Athens would harm his image as a true Hellene.

To Thebes, his former ally, Philip showed no such generosity. He broke up the Boeotian federation, long dominated by Thebes, restored the destroyed cities of Plataea and Orchomenus and put a Macedonian garrison in Thebes' citadel, the Cadmaea, to support a narrow pro-Macedonian oligarchy.

MERCY TO SPARTA
To that other once great city, Sparta, Philip behaved differently. When the Spartans refused to send envoys to the Council of Corinth, saying they were accustomed to lead other Greeks, not follow them, Philip invaded Laconia. He seemed about to take Sparta – this would not have been difficult, as Sparta's army was tiny – but desisted.

He knew that Sparta still appeared to menace her smaller neighbours, making them pro-Macedonian. He simply ravaged Sparta's lands and reduced her territory still further, giving the Dentheliatis border area to Messenia, Sparta's

Below: Found in the royal tombs at Vergina (ancient Aegae, the old capital), this silver vase reveals the wealth and sophistication Macedonia attained under Philip II.

Above: Philip was the first Greek ruler to mint coins in gold, such as this stater showing the god Apollo. He could do so thanks to his acquisition of the gold mines of Mt Pangaeus.

worst enemy. Then he called a Panhellenic Council at Corinth in the winter of 338–337 BC.

Philip chose Corinth partly because of its central position and wealth but mainly because of its associations. It had been the seat of the Panhellenic League in the Persian Wars almost 150 years earlier, when many Greek states had for once united against Persia. Isocrates (436–338 BC), the Athenian writer, had long urged the Greeks to stop fighting each other and turn against Persia, inside whose supposedly decaying empire they could easily win booty and new lands. He now hailed Philip as fulfilling his idea of a Panhellenic crusade.

A COMMON PEACE
Philip, happy to accept the aged orator's praise, had his own reasons for a Persian campaign, but first he had to settle affairs in Greece. Elected Captain-General of all

the Greeks, a novel post, he announced a Common Peace. Superficially, this promised an end to Greece's incessant feuds by guaranteeing existing constitutions and banning any redistribution of land. Actually, as pro-Macedonian oligarchs had taken over in many places, it meant that he controlled much of Greece. To reinforce his hold, Philip stationed garrisons in Corinth, Ambracia and Chalcis (in Euboea), besides Thebes. Philip then announced a Panhellenic war of revenge, sent Parmenion ahead with 10,000 troops into Asia and returned north. Before he conquered Asia, there were domestic affairs to deal with.

ASSASSINATION

"Wounded is the bull; the end is near; the sacrificer is at hand." So spoke the Delphic oracle, ambiguous as ever, in response to Philip's enquiries. Flushed with success, Philip assumed the bull to be the Persian Empire. In the summer of 336BC at Aegae he celebrated the marriage of his young daughter Cleopatra to her uncle Alexander of Epirus. Such close ties were acceptable among royalty, for it was certainly no love match. In 338BC Philip himself, however, had fallen in love with and married 17-year-old Eurydice, niece of his general Attalus. She produced a daughter and then, in 336BC, a son. Philip promptly divorced Olympias, whose Epirote connections were no longer needed, making Alexander deeply worried about his future.

That wedding day, however, when Philip watched the procession of the Twelve Olympian gods at Aegae, followed by his own image in Olympian size, he was flanked by both Alexanders: his son and his new son-in-law. Suddenly a young guard called Pausanias rushed up and stabbed Philip, who died instantly. Pausanias, caught as he tried to escape, was summarily executed.

The true motive behind the murder died with him – conveniently for many people, perhaps. The story went that Pausanias, once Philip's lover, had been raped by

Left: Isocrates (436–338BC) was an Athenian orator who had long called for Greece to unite against Persia. In his last years he hailed Philip as the ideal leader for such a Panhellenic crusade.

servants of Attalus, whom he had slandered. Why Pausanias should then want to murder the king is unclear. What is clear is who benefited: Alexander, Philip's son by Olympias, due to be left behind in the coming war on Persia, and Olympias, Philip's ex-wife in bitter exile. Politics in Macedonia seemed to be reverting to their chaotic norm. But Philip, although cheated of winning an Asian empire, had built his kingdom so solidly that it did not fall apart. This was his real achievement.

Below: This elaborately decorated gold lamax or coffin found in the royal tombs at Vergina (ancient Aegae) contains what may be Philip II's bones. Such flamboyant riches recalled the splendours of Mycenaean Greece, the age of heroes, not of the cash-strapped democracies then the norm in Greece proper.

CHAPTER II

THE YOUNG ALEXANDER

356–336BC

Alexander was a phenomenon from birth – or so it was later told. The stories of his early years are so colourful that they approach the legendary. But there is no doubt that he was an infant and then adolescent prodigy. Remarkably precocious, he tamed a savage stallion at the age of 12 and was left as regent of the kingdom in his father Philip II's absence when only 16, repelling an invasion and founding his first city. When just 18 he led the decisive cavalry charge at the Battle of Chaeronea and then a delicate diplomatic mission to Athens.

Life in the Macedonian court – stimulating, exhilarating, never easy – encouraged rapid developers, but only a year later Alexander's position as heir apparent seemed endangered by Philip's last marriage. A year after that, he found himself king at the age of 20, ascending the throne over his father's corpse. What involvement if any he had in Philip's murder is unknown, but his succession was far from inevitable. Yet southern Greeks who confidently expected Macedonia to collapse into its traditional feuding after the death of Philip were soon disappointed. Within weeks Alexander was master of his own kingdom; within months he had made a lightning descent through Greece, claiming Philip's powers and titles. The Balkan campaign that followed, and the blitzkrieg return that destroyed Thebes, showed the Greeks that he was already even more dangerous than Philip.

Left: Lion hunt mosaic of c.310BC from Pella showing the young Alexander hunting lions.

BIRTH AND CHILDHOOD
356–347 BC

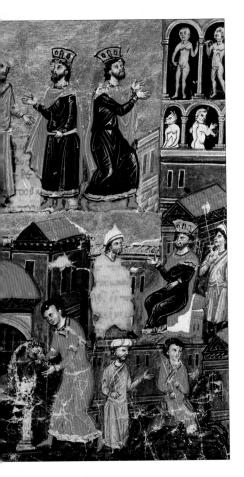

The baby who became Alexander III, Alexander the Great, was born in July 356 BC to Olympias, daughter of the royal house of Epirus, and Philip II of Macedonia. According to Plutarch, before his birth Olympias dreamt that lightning struck her womb, while Philip dreamt that her womb showed a lion's seal. Philip received the news of the birth of his first (legitimate) son on the same day his horses won at the Olympic Games and his troops took Potidaea. Philip's Temenid family claimed descent via Hercules

Left: Two scenes from The Romance of Alexander, *a fantastical history written about Alexander long after his death. Here it shows Alexander consulting the Delphic Oracle (above), which is a fiction, and with his horse Bucephalus (below), who existed.*

from Zeus, whose mountain home rose abruptly on their kingdom's southern flanks. Olympias' family traced its descent from Achilles, Homer's heroic prince. So Alexander had the most illustrious forebears imaginable. This helped shape his exalted view of his destiny.

Little is known of Alexander's childhood. The young prince could not have seen much of his father, who was away on his wars. His mother chose his first two tutors. One of them was her cousin Leonidas, who emulated his Spartan namesake, hero of Thermopylae, in toughness and austerity, confiscating anything exotic or luxurious in Alexander's belongings. When Alexander later conquered the Lebanon, he sent wagonloads of incense to Leonidas, telling him not to be mean to the gods. By contrast, kind old Lysimachus became so attached to Alexander that he followed him to Asia.

Such sober male influences countered the erratic behaviour of Alexander's mother. Olympias reputedly kept sacred snakes in her bed and worshipped Dionysus, god of wine and orgies, and the sinister Hecate, goddess of suicide and the underworld. "While others sacrifice tens and hundreds of animals, Olympias sacrifices them by the thousand and tens of thousand," wrote a student of Aristotle, the philosopher who came to know the intrigues and personalities at the court at Pella well.

NEW ARRIVALS AT PELLA
Pella was growing fast at this time, as Philip's conquests attracted diplomats, courtiers, artists, merchants and exiles. Among the last was the Persian Artabazus,

Left: The birth of Alexander in 356 BC, shown in this mosaic of c.310 BC from Phoenicia, was preceded by portents of greatness, according to later legends. Phoenicia was a part of Asia that became Hellenized after his conquest.

a former satrap of Phrygia. He brought with him Barsine, his beautiful young daughter, ten years older than Alexander. Alexander talked to Persians with friendly curiosity, discovering the virtues of this civilized people. Years later, when they met again in Asia, Alexander reappointed Artabazus as satrap, while Barsine became one of his mistresses. Many newcomers to Pella were southern Greeks: Nearchus the sailor from Crete, Demaratus the soldier from Corinth. All became Alexander's lifelong friends, although most Macedonians looked down on Greek hirelings.

THE PEACE CONFERENCE

In 346BC Philip's combination of guile, cash and force led to his triumph. Macedonian armies entered central Greece ostensibly to 'punish' Phocian sacrilege. For the resulting peace conference at Pella emissaries came from all over Greece, including two from Athens: Demosthenes and his opponent Aeschines, probably in Philip's pay.

By then Alexander was ten, old enough to appear and "play the lyre and recite and debate with another boy", according to Aeschines. A year later a row blew up in Athens amid accusations that one or other of the politicians had flirted with the already handsome young prince and been unduly influenced by him.

Whatever the truth, it suggests that Alexander was already politically alert and also reveals the prevalence of homosexuality in Greek public life.

Above: A view of Mt Olympus, the mountain home of the Olympian gods. Alexander came to believe that he was indeed the son of Zeus, king of the gods.

BUCEPHALUS: ALEXANDER'S HORSE

When Alexander was twelve, he began one of the greatest relationships in his life – with a horse. His friend Demaratus had offered Philip a huge black stallion costing 13 talents, more than three times anything paid for a horse before. Philip ordered the horse to be led out but it bucked and reared, refusing all orders. Philip was about to reject it when Alexander offered to tame him. Taking the horse by his halter, Alexander patted and quieted him. Then he mounted and galloped around to universal applause, Philip exclaiming proudly that Macedonia would never contain such a boy. Or so the story goes. Alexander had noticed that the horse was shying at its own shadow. By turning its head to the sun, he overcame its fears.

Alexander called his horse Bucephalus, 'Ox-head', because of a white mark on his black head. Bucephalus became devoted to his royal master, following him literally to the ends of the Earth. Alexander rode him in his greatest battles and taught him to kneel fully armoured before him. When hill tribes near the Caspian Sea kidnapped the horse, Alexander's anger was so terrible that they returned him at once.

Alexander last rode Bucephalus into battle against the Indian rajah Porus in 326BC. Soon after, Bucephalus died of old age, being perhaps 30. (The Greeks did not know how to tell a horse's age by its teeth, the standard method.) Alexander commemorated his beloved stallion by founding and naming a city after him in what is now northern Pakistan.

Below: Alexander astride Bucephalus, the black stallion he rode to the ends of the Earth. Alexander was above all a cavalry commander.

EDUCATION AND YOUTH
346–340 BC

Above: Aristotle, once Plato's most brilliant student in the Academy in Athens, was chosen by Philip to tutor the young prince. If unheroic in appearance, Aristotle had much the greatest mind of his generation, widening Alexander's mental horizons.

Below: A medieval painting of Aristotle's school for Alexander and his companions at Mieza, where he taught the boys subjects from zoology to drama.

Alexander had only one full sibling, his young sister Cleopatra, of whom he was very fond. But Macedonian girls played little part in public life, although they were not as secluded as those in Athens. To prepare his precocious, intelligent but emotionally volatile son for public affairs, Philip encouraged noblemen's sons to join what became the select group of Alexander's close companions. Foremost among these was Hephaistion, son of Amyntor, a Macedonian aristocrat.

HEPHAISTION

Alexander, who had learned to read when very young, was obsessed throughout his life by Homer's great poems, especially *The Iliad*, which related the exploits of his irascible supposed ancestor Achilles. In *The Iliad* Achilles is passionately devoted to his friend Patroclus, a devotion that by the 4th century BC was widely seen as erotic, although this is not how Homer shows it. Almost certainly Alexander and Hephaistion were lovers,

then and for years after, although Alexander always said that only sex and sleep reminded him that he was mortal. A homosexual relationship between the two boys would have been thought acceptable, even laudable, in Macedonia's militaristic society.

The one surviving portrait of Hephaistion does not suggest great beauty, and records indicate an utterly loyal, if rather dull, subordinate, who ended his career as Alexander's Grand Vizier. Dull but devoted loyalty was what Alexander needed at this stage, however, for his parents were constantly quarrelling. Philip was taking other, younger wives, often for reasons of state, making Olympias ragingly jealous. Alexander must have been the unhappy recipient of her hysterical rants.

Olympias reputedly also introduced a Thessalian prostitute into Alexander's bedroom to test his virility. Understandably, he rejected her – all his life Alexander hated prostitution or rape.

Other boys from the Macedonian nobility, including two sons of Antipater (one of Philip's best generals) and some from Upper Macedonian clans, notably Harpalus, joined the magic circle, soon guided by the age's greatest mind. For Philip wanted the best tutor money could buy for his adolescent son. In 342BC he chose another north Greek: Aristotle.

THE PHILOSOPHER-TUTOR

Born in 384BC in Stagira, a small city in the Chalcidice recently deleted by Macedonia, Aristotle had been the most brilliant student at Plato's Academy in Athens. He had left Athens on Plato's death in 347BC, probably disappointed at not being chosen as the next head of the Academy. Going north to the Troad (Dardanelles), he joined a community of philosophers and soon married the daughter of Hermias, a local ruler, at whose court he then lived. He later joined the polymath Theophrastus on Lesbos, where he carried out zoological investigations. So he was no reclusive academic (if unheroically "thin-legged and small-eyed") when he landed in Macedonia in 342BC to teach the 14-year-old prince. He stayed for four years based at Mieza, a small coastal town.

"[Aristotle] taught him writing, Greek, Hebrew, Babylonian and Latin. He taught him the nature of the winds and sea; he explained the stars' courses, the revolutions of the heaven.... He showed him justice and rhetoric and warned him against the looser sort of women." This comes from *The Romance of Alexander*, a most unreliable biography. Neither Aristotle nor Alexander learned Hebrew, Babylonian or even Latin (Rome was still struggling for survival in central Italy, although Aristotle, hearing of it, noted that it had the institutions of a *polis*). But Aristotle did teach Alexander a huge amount about the natural world.

Bertrand Russell, the 20th-century philosopher, thought that Alexander must have been "bored by the prosy old pedant". However, Aristotle had courtly

Right: A giant bronze head of Hephaistion, Alexander's first friend and very probably first lover. Hephaistion became Alexander's trusted second-in-command, his death causing the king huge grief.

manners – his father Nicomachus had been physician to Amyntas III, Philip's predecessor – and at only 42 was not old. Alexander's interests in botany, zoology, geography and biology were fired by Aristotle, and he later sent specimens from Asia back to his old tutor. Aristotle also deepened his knowledge of Greek literature, especially of the great Athenian playwrights, Euripides becoming one of Alexander's favourite authors. But the boy grew into a man of action, not thought, probably never much interested in Aristotle's ethics or metaphysics.

GREEKS AND BARBARIANS

On one point they differed profoundly. Aristotle had the typical Greek prejudices about 'barbarians', meaning all non-Greeks, including Persians. He considered them inherently inferior, to be treated as slaves. Quite early in his career, Alexander began thinking and behaving differently. This led him ultimately to clash with his own soldiers – and with Callisthenes, Aristotle's relative who was appointed as Alexander's official historian. Yet Aristotle must have widened and enriched Alexander's view of the world. Aristotle was enriched in the worldly sense by his stay in Macedonia. When Aristotle died in 322BC, he had 18 slaves – the sign of a rich man and unusual for a philosopher.

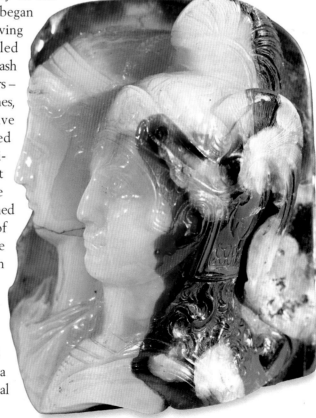

Below: Olympias, shown here in a cameo portrait with her son Alexander, was a stormy character, frequently clashing with her unfaithful husband and trying to turn her son against the king. Alexander inherited much of her fiery temperament and mysticism.

FIRST COMMANDS AND FAMILY QUARRELS 340–336BC

Above: Epirus on the north-western fringes of Greece was even wilder than Macedonia. It was the home of Olympias, to which she retreated after being divorced by Philip. Alexander, who had quarrelled with his father, accompanied her but soon returned.

Far more central to Alexander's upbringing than studying botany or even Homer was his military training. All Macedonian boys learned the basics of arms drill and riding while young. By his teens Alexander was as good at riding and using arms as could be hoped. He was also a passionate hunter, pursuing the bears, lions and boars found in Macedonia's forests – a traditional royal pastime. What could not be known in advance, and could hardly be taught, was the knack of leadership, vital in the informal but absolute monarchy of Macedonia.

THE DEFEAT OF THE MAEDI

While Philip was away campaigning in Thrace and then engaged in the long, ultimately fruitless sieges of Perinthus and Byzantium in 340BC, Alexander was left as regent. This reveals Philip's confidence in a son still only aged 16, although his experienced general Antipater was on hand to give advice if needed. Alexander's military skill was tested almost at once, for an invasion by a Thracian people called the Maedi (who may have heard of the king's absence) threatened Macedonia's eastern borders. Gathering

the reserves, Alexander marched forth and defeated the Maedi, pursuing them back into Thrace. To commemorate his victory, he founded a city he called Alexandropolis, the first city of many to bear his name.

BATTLE OF CHAERONEA

What Philip, who had founded only two cities himself, thought of this is not recorded, but he was clearly impressed enough by his son's military skill to give Alexander command of the cavalry on the left wing of the Macedonian army at the Battle of Chaeronea in 338BC. This was a battle mostly fought between, and decided by, hoplites. Alexander's well-timed charge cut off the amateur Athenian infantry from their Theban allies. He then turned on the more experienced Thebans, keeping them surrounded until the Macedonian infantry caught up and destroyed them. (Greek cavalry was generally ineffectual against well-trained hoplite infantry.) Alexander had shown that he could lead horsemen in a dashing charge *and* control them.

Shortly afterwards Philip appointed Alexander to lead the guard of honour that ceremoniously returned the ashes of Athens' dead soldiers to the city – something essential to Greek burial rites. As a special guest, Alexander was shown around Greece's greatest city. He reputedly turned down the offer of a young boy as company for his bed, again showing his dislike of prostitution. What he thought of Athens itself, which even Plato, who had very mixed feelings about his native city, had called "the city hall of Greek wisdom", is unknown.

QUARRELS AND EXILE

This harmony between father and son did not last. Back in Macedonia, Philip married for the seventh time, his bride

Below: Alexander and a friend, perhaps Craterus, hunting lions, in a mosaic from Pella of c.310BC. Alexander loved hunting almost as much as war, although he did neither naked.

this time being the 17-year-old Eurydice, great niece of Attalus, one of his leading marshals. Unlike many of Philip's politically motivated earlier marriages, this time he was in love. Worryingly for Alexander, Eurydice's children would be full Macedonians, not half-Epirote like himself. One drunken night Attalus invited the company to pray for "a true Macedonian heir". Alexander, enraged and flushed with drink, caused a row. His father, also drunk, staggered up drawing his sword but stumbled and fell. "Here is the man who would cross to Asia but falls between the couches!" jeered Alexander. Taking his mother and close companions, he went into exile in Epirus.

Olympias remained in exile until Philip's death. But Philip still needed an adult heir, while Alexander soon grew bored in provincial Epirus and wanted to return home. Accordingly, within months things were patched up between father and son, the reconciliation helped by Eurydice's first child being a girl. Alexander remained nervous about his position, however, as was demonstrated by the Carian marriage fiasco.

THE CARIAN MARRIAGE FIASCO

Arrhidaeus was Philip's half-witted son by a dancing-girl. Such a minor royal was good enough to offer as a husband for the daughter of the Carian satrap, who wanted to ally himself with Philip, thus usefully extending Philip's influence into Asia. However, Alexander, hearing of this, secretly proposed himself as a husband instead, fearing that Philip was preparing to give his kingdom to Arrhidaeus. The delighted Carians accepted the prospect of the much more impressive Alexander until Philip vetoed the plan, exiling many of Alexander's friends who had convinced him to take this action. Taking fright, the Carians then sought a match with a Persian satrap, so wrecking Philip's carefully laid plans.

THE DEATH OF PHILIP

In 336BC Eurydice gave birth to a boy, a rival to Alexander. That same summer Philip announced the marriage of Cleopatra, his daughter by Olympias, to Alexander of Epirus, her uncle. This marriage meant that Philip no longer needed a marriage tie with Olympias, whom he promptly divorced. Alexander again felt insecure, especially as he would be left behind as regent when Philip invaded Asia. But he accompanied his father that fateful morning in August 336BC into the theatre at Aegae to watch the procession of the Olympian gods. Within minutes Philip was dead, assassinated for unknown reasons by Pausanias, a bodyguard. Alexander was the obvious heir. But his succession was by no means automatic.

Above: In this excellent copy of a bust by Lysippus, one of the age's finest sculptors, the visionary dynamism and ruthlessness of the young conqueror are apparent.

SECURING THE THRONE AND GREECE 336–335BC

Above: The wealth of Macedonia is revealed by this gold-decorated breastplate found in the royal tombs at Vergina (ancient Aegae), dating from Philip II's reign.

Below: The fine Ionic columns of the royal palace at Pella, the capital where Alexander spent his last winter in Macedonia in 335–334BC.

Although he was the obvious heir, Alexander's succession was not assured. His cousin Amyntas, shouldered aside 20 years before, had a claim to the throne, as had Eurydice's infant son. But Alexander was known to the army and nobility. When Alexander of Lyncestis stepped forward to hail Alexander as king, things moved his way. The assassin Pausanias, caught as he fled to a waiting horse, was speedily executed. So too were Amyntas, Eurydice's son and two Lyncestid brothers whose loyalty was suspect. Such precautionary ferocity became a hallmark of his reign. Alexander announced a timely tax cut and organized funeral games for his father. Philip was buried in royal splendour in tombs that have only recently been discovered.

At first Alexander could count on the firm support of only one of Philip's three marshals, Antipater. Of the two others, he had Attalus, his enemy, who was commanding the advance guard in Asia, quietly murdered. This was done with the consent of Parmenion, the last of the three. (Parmenion's sons were serving with Alexander, making them useful hostages.) With the throne secure, he led the army between the two halves of a dissected dog – an old Macedonian rite – and then turned south in October.

Greece was in ferment. News of Philip's murder had raised anti-Macedonians' hopes everywhere, and Alexander had to quash them quickly. As Thessaly refused to let him pass through the Vale of Tempe, he cut steps in the side of Mt Ossa to bypass it, being duly elected leader by the astonished Thessalians, henceforth faithful allies. Bursting into Greece at the head of his army, he deflated opposition, being elected head of the League of Corinth in succession to Philip. Then he turned north. Before he left for Asia, there were Balkan tribes to be pacified.

THE BALKANS – AND THEBES

His first target in 335BC was the Triballians, a Thracian people who had ambushed Philip three years before. Finding the crucial Shipka Pass defended by Triballians holding carts poised to roll down on his army, he ordered his men to lie flat on the ground with their shields over them. The carts rumbled past harmlessly above and Alexander resumed the attack, using slingers and archers to lure the Triballians into the open, where his infantry crushed them. The Triballians then retreated to the River Danube's far banks. Alexander lacked ships to ferry his whole army across, so the Macedonians filled their leather tents with straw and crossed the river on these impromptu rafts, protected by catapult fire. Forming up on the other side, they routed the amazed Triballians, some of whom joined this increasingly polyglot army. Alexander was the first Greek commander to cross the Danube.

Alexander next moved against the Illyrians on the north-west frontier. Getting trapped in a narrow wooded valley, he formed a phalanx 120 deep. With its massed sarissas making a terrible swishing sound and its shields clashing, he routed the Illyrians by fear rather than arms. A later night attack had completed their defeat when news from the south required his rapid return: Thebes had revolted on

Above: A romantic depiction of Alexander's triumphs by the 19th-century artist Gustave Moreau. Alexander's lightning conquests soon passed into legend.

DIOGENES AND ALEXANDER

Diogenes of Sinope (404–325BC) was a most original philosopher. Despising worldly goods, he slept in a tub and performed all bodily functions in public. He believed that only one thing mattered: distinguishing between virtue and vice. His scorn for convention won him the nickname *cynos* (dog), and his followers were known as Cynics. Reputedly, when visiting Corinth in 336BC, he met Alexander. Was there, the king asked, anything he could do for him? Yes, said Diogenes, get out of my sunlight. Impressed, Alexander said that if he had not been Alexander, he would have chosen to be Diogenes. Certainly both men pursued their aims with single-minded extremism.

Below: At Corinth, busy organizing the Panhellenic League against Persia, Alexander encountered the ascetic Cynic philosopher Diogenes living in a tub.

rumours that Alexander was dead, killing some Macedonian officers and restoring its democracy.

In two weeks Alexander marched his army 800km/500 miles south – an unbelievably fast pace. The Thebans at first could not believe it, but when they did, they were defiant,. However, no help came from any other Greeks. In the resulting battle outside the city the Macedonians were hard-pressed at first, but the Thebans left a side gate open behind them. The Macedonians pushed through it and Thebes fell to them. All its 35,000 inhabitants were killed or enslaved and all its buildings, except the temples and the house of Pindar, its famous poet, destroyed. One of Greece's most ancient cities was no more.

After this act of calculated terror, which the League of Corinth rubber-stamped, Alexander had no further problems with the Greeks. He demanded but did not get Demosthenes from Athens, instead taking 20 Athenian triremes as hostages. Then he returned home to prepare for invasion by a winter of feasting and planning.

AIMS AND STRENGTHS
334 BC

Above: This elaborate krater *(drinking vessel) of gilded bronze from Macedonia illustrates the kingdom's recently acquired wealth.*

Below: Alexander, here shown on the Sidon Sarcophagus *carved soon after his death, always led his armies from the front in battle.*

Alexander was not the first Greek ruler to conceive of attacking the Persian Empire. Jason of Pherae and Philip, his father, had both had invasion plans, aborted only by their murders, and the idea had been suggested by Isocrates among others for decades. The 'March of the 10,000' – the Greek mercenaries who had penetrated the Persian Empire and returned almost unharmed in 401 BC – appeared to show up the vulnerability of Persia. Persia had regularly hired Greek hoplites ever since, who continued to dominate warfare around the Mediterranean and in Egypt. But the unsuccessful campaigns of the Spartan king Agesilaus in Asia Minor in the 390s BC indicated that conquering Asia needed more than just a decent general and hoplites. (Problems back in Greece had called Agesilaus home anyway.) If Persia lacked heavy infantry to match Greek hoplites, it had fine cavalry in abundance.

AN UNKNOWN EMPIRE
Few Greeks had any idea of what an eastern campaign might entail. While some had visited Susa, the administrative capital (in south-western Iran) as envoys, mercenaries, captives or craftsmen, none realized the empire's true immensity. Even Aristotle, who probably knew more geography than any other Greek, vastly underestimated the distance between the Aegean and Susa. And the Iranian heartland of the empire stretched east of Susa. To traverse the broad plateaux and mountain ranges of Asia and so conquer Persia, cavalry was needed in force, backed by an army that was professional in every department.

STRONG ARMY, WEAK NAVY
Alexander had such an army, thanks to Philip, for the first time in Greek history, based on the infantry grouped into massive phalanxes that were invincible in the right conditions. He also had the commando-style Shield Bearers, siege engines and catapults, Cretan archers and Thracian and Illyrian irregulars as slingers and javelin-throwers. Above all he had excellent cavalry, including some Thessalians, who had taught the Macedonians their highly effective wedge-attack formations.

In 334 BC, after Alexander had crossed into Asia, he fielded about 43,000 infantry and 6,000 cavalry – by Greek standards a huge army, though modest by Persian. Alexander left Antipater in Macedonia with another force of 12,000 infantry and 1,500 cavalry, plus garrison troops across Greece and the Macedonian Empire. The gold and silver from Mt Pangaeus, coupled with the lands newly conquered by Philip and worked by slave labour, helped to pay for all this. Even so, he started his campaign in May 334 BC 600 talents in debt.

The one major Macedonian weakness was its lack of a decent navy: it had only 160 triremes, including its unwilling allies. Athens had 400 triremes, although it lacked the needed sailors. This was the biggest Greek fleet, but Athens was ambivalently neutral. The 20 Athenian ships Alexander took acted chiefly as hostages in the fleet, most of which he dismissed anyway in 334 BC.

Ultimately, Alexander's greatest asset was his own genius and luck, in which he believed from the start and which his men soon came to accept. Good generals and the best army in the world were his tangible strengths.

AN EVOLVING PLAN
What exact aim Alexander had in mind when he began his attack in spring 334 BC remains debatable. The historian William Tarn wrote: "The primary reason Alexander invaded Persia was that he never thought

of *not* doing so. It was his inheritance." Alexander's declared purpose in 334BC was to exact revenge on Persia for its invasion of 480–479BC. Most Greeks, however, did not see this as his real reason. Probably, like some of his officers, they expected Alexander simply to conquer Asia Minor, raid the Persian heartland and return with loot. Rivalry with his dead father – a semi-conscious desire to conquer more rapidly and completely than Philip had – may have spurred Alexander on at first, but his *pothos* (longing) and an increasingly imperial vision led him ever further east.

ALEXANDER THE ASIAN EMPEROR

On landing in Asia, Alexander threw a spear on to the shore, symbolically claiming the empire by right of conquest. He then appointed a Macedonian as satrap of coastal Phrygia, the first province conquered, seeming to continue the Persian imperial system. Soon after, however, he posed as liberator of the Greek cities in Asia Minor, and later sent back to Athens from Susa the statues of Harmodius and Aristogeiton, the Athenian tyrannicides, carried off in 480BC. But he began reappointing Persians as satraps to rule their provinces after Gaugamela in 331BC, his greatest victory. By then he was seeing himself as heir to the Achaemenids, the rulers of Asia. As such, he had to impress his Asian subjects,

and he began wearing elements of Persian royal dress and adopting Persian court customs such as *proskynesis*, bowing to the throne. Such innovations proved very unpopular with his Macedonians. Alexander, who had started the war as a Greek avenger, ended it as a Greek-speaking Asian emperor.

Above: Alexander at the charge. He loved warfare more than anything else, having a truly Homeric delight in battle.

Left: The phalanx remained a vital part of Alexander's army, although in battle he usually relied on cavalry to deliver the knockout blow.

PERSIA: AN EMPIRE IN DECLINE? 404–336BC

The Achaemenid Empire created by Cyrus the Great and Darius I (556–486BC) was the greatest power on Earth, ruling all lands between the Indus and Macedonia. The Greeks in the Persian Wars (490–478BC) had managed to defeat Persia only by an unusual display of unity. It then took the fleet of Athens and her allies in the Delian Confederacy years of hard fighting to clear the Aegean islands and coasts of Persian bases. When Athens tried to interfere in Cyprus and Egypt, she was crushingly defeated.

The Peace of Callias of 449BC had definitively confirmed that the Aegean islands and cities would be Athenian, while the rest of Asia, including half-Greek Cyprus, would be Persian, as would Egypt, the second richest satrapy in the empire. Athens in truth had stripped Persia of only a few coastal cities.

Below: The Apadana Staircase at Persepolis, built under Darius I (521–486BC), showing the 10,000 Immortals, the elite royal Foot Guards so-called because when one died, he was immediately replaced.

TREACHERY AT COURT

Persian power depended finally on the Great King, who in turn depended on his courtiers. Artaxerxes III had made Bagoas, a eunuch, his Grand Vizier (first minister) – eunuchs were often employed at court because they were thought to present no threat. Bagoas had ideas of his own, however, and in 338BC he poisoned his royal master, as he did the next king. Bagoas then chose Darius Codomanus, a nobleman with only a distant claim to the throne, as the next ruler. In 336BC he became king as Darius III, the last Achaemenid. Darius promptly had the treacherous eunuch killed; but he was to prove no match for Alexander, who became king that same year.

EGYPTIAN INDEPENDENCE

Egypt, however, proudly conscious of its ancient civilization, was never happy under Persian rule. Its *fellahin* (peasants) were swayed by its powerful priests, who were angered by obvious Persian contempt for their religion. As a result, Egypt revolted frequently. It rebelled three times in the 5th century BC and after 405BC was independent for 60 years, relying on Greek hoplites to repel the Persians. These included King Agesilaus of Sparta in his cash-strapped old age.

Egyptian independence was a humiliation as well as a financial loss for the Great King, but not a serious threat to the Persian Empire in the way that the revolt of Prince Cyrus in 401BC was. Jealous of his older brother Artaxerxes, who had just succeeded to the throne, Cyrus had had unusually wide powers in Asia Minor. He used them to recruit a rebel army, whose core consisted of 'The 10,000' Greek hoplites, and 'marched upcountry' (as recorded in soldier-turned-historian Xenophon's work *Anabasis*). Persian imperial forces did not try to check his passage until he reached Cunaxa, just north of Babylon. The rebels won the ensuing battle, thanks mainly to the Greeks. But Cyrus, who had personally tried to kill his detested brother, was killed. The subsequent return home of the Greeks under Xenophon's command made a colourful tale, and it taught the Persians the need to hire Greek hoplites. This was easy for the wealthy empire. The real problem was the satraps.

THE REVOLT OF THE SATRAPS

The Persian system of government gave satraps remarkably wide powers, both financial and military, over their often large provinces. The size and diversity of the Persian Empire and the slowness of communications perhaps made such devolution inevitable, and the 'King's Ears', as the royal agents were known, acted as a check. But in the distant reaches of the empire (western Asia Minor was a full three months' march from Susa even on the Royal Road) satraps tended to establish hereditary dynasties. These semi-ducal rulers developed local ties, ambitions and rivalries that could undermine loyalty to the crown in distant Susa.

In the 360s BC many satrapies in western Asia rose in what has been called the 'Revolt of the Satraps'. Even Cappadocia in the Anatolian interior rebelled, as did Cyprus (again) and Sidon in Phoenicia. In Caria the dynast Mausolus began to extend his power, while Egypt remained independent. Since coins, essential to pay mercenaries, were minted only in western satrapies, this loss threatened the Persians' recruitment of essential Greek mercenaries and of its fleet, mostly supplied by Phoenicia, Cyprus and Caria. The whole empire west of the Euphrates appeared lost.

In 358BC Artaxerxes II, an incompetent drunk, was succeeded by Artaxerxes III Ochus, a far better ruler. Like Philip II,

Above: Two of the 10,000 Immortals, Persian noblemen who formed the Foot Guards. They were, however, the only heavy infantry the Great King had at his disposal.

Below: A gold winged-lion rhyton (drinking vessel) of the 6th century BC, emblematic of the splendour and wealth of the Persian empire.

his contemporary, Artaxerxes played off his enemies against each other, while mustering immense forces from the Persian heartlands. With them he crushed Artabazus, satrap of coastal Phrygia (north-western Asia Minor) and began regaining the whole peninsula, helped by the death of Mausolus in 353BC. In 344BC Persia recaptured Sidon after a long siege and went on to regain Egypt, although brutal reprisals there made its rule hated. By 340BC Persian power in the west had been fully restored, it seemed, and Artaxerxes could help the cities of Perinthus and Byzantium when Philip besieged them.

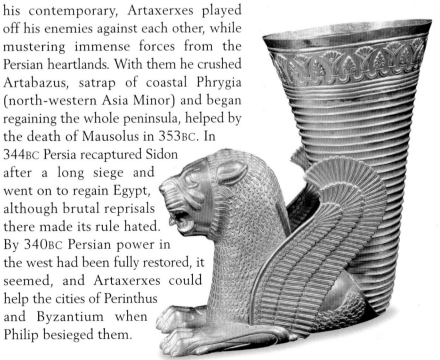

PERSIA: STRENGTHS AND STRATEGY 335–333 BC

Above: By the 330s BC, the Persian empire had amassed 230,000 talents in its royal treasuries at Susa and Persepolis. Only a tiny fraction of the gold mountain was made into fine gold rhytons such as this.

The Greeks in the 4th century BC generally underestimated Persian power, their views shaped not just by the March of 'The 10,000' but by broader Greek prejudices about 'barbarians' as inherently inferior beings. But Persia remained the superpower of its age, though perhaps one with clay feet. From only a day's march inland (*c*.48km/30 miles) from the Aegean coast eastward, the Great King's power remained substantially intact. Along the Royal Road that ran nearly 2,400km/1,500 miles from Sardis to Susa

messengers still galloped, bearing satraps' reports to the empire's capitals and returning with royal edicts. Babylonia, the empire's richest province and home to the earliest civilization, lay sheltered in its arc, supplying the food and other raw materials vital to the empire. The Phoenician cities, which provided professional fleets of 300 or more galleys, likewise remained under Persian suzerainty. Egypt had recently been regained and Caria and Cyprus were once more under control. None of these cities or peoples was pro-Persian but, with the exception of Egypt, none was strongly anti-Persian either. Imperial rule was usually sufficiently flexible and tolerant not to alienate its subjects.

MILITARY STRENGTHS ...

But the core of the empire remained the Iranian peoples: the Medes and the Persians, devoted to the throne and the empire, if not always to the king himself. They were united also by their common Zoroastrian religion. The Great King was not regarded as a god by the quasi-monotheistic Persians, but his role and power were seen as divinely sanctioned, under the special protection of Ahura Mazda, the Wise Lord.

Persian boys were traditionally taught to ride, shoot straight and never tell a lie. The result was very capable, tough horsemen and excellent archers. Persian archers' composite bow could fire arrows 183 metres/200 yards, and the home province of Persis (Fars) alone potentially provided 30,000 archers. On the lush pastures of Media around Ecbatana 200,000 heavy Nisaean horses grazed,

Left: A Lydian leading horses, from a relief in Darius I's palace in Persepolis. The peoples of all western Asia contributed to Persia's massive military strength.

Above: Persian power finally depended on the Great King and the last Achaemenid ruler. Darius III, pictured in his chariot, proved to be no general or even warrior when he faced Alexander.

ready to supply mounts for the 120,00 or so cavalry that the Great King could almost immediately call upon.

... AND WEAKNESSES

Only in infantry were the Persians at a disadvantage. They had 'The 10,000' foot guards, called 'Immortals' because (reputedly) the moment one died he was replaced by another. But for their other heavy infantry they had long turned to Greece. There were said, with only small exaggeration, to be 50,000 Greek mercenaries fighting on the Persian side in the two main battles, more than all the troops in Alexander's army. They proved generally loyal to their paymasters.

DISTANT THREATS

East of Media, across the high plateaux of eastern Iran and Central Asia, ran the Khorasan Highway, not a paved military road but a time-honoured route for merchants as well as armies, stretching to Bactria and Sogdiana (today Uzbekistan) in Central Asia. North of these satrapies lay arid empty steppes from which savage nomads could suddenly emerge.

These had long posed a far greater threat to the Persian heartland than Greek sailors scudding around the Aegean like pirates.

NO FIXED STRATEGY

Gold and silver tribute, from Egypt to Sogdiana, had flowed for two centuries into the royal treasuries at Susa and Persepolis, the grand ceremonial centre, creating a gigantic reserve of 230,000 talents – riches beyond the dreams of any Greek power. But all still depended vitally on the king. Darius III, although he had killed a man in single combat and was imposingly handsome, proved neither a good strategist nor a competent field commander. Twice at vital moments in battle he was to panic and flee, giving Alexander victory. Such physical cowardice or loss of nerve would have mattered less if he had remained behind the front. But Persian kings were generally expected to lead their armies

Faced with an aggressive invader, Persia could have tried to stop Alexander's army from crossing the Hellespont in 334BC, but the inferior Macedonian fleet was unopposed. They were then faced with a choice: confront Alexander head on in battle or wear him out by a scorched-earth policy, retreating east into Asia while trying to raise revolts at his rear to cut him off. Greece was full of men unhappy with Macedonian hegemony, and Persia had the money to finance revolts. This was the strategy advocated by Memnon, the mercenary from Rhodes who had risen high in Persian service, marrying a Persian wife and being granted estates in Asia Minor. His advice was at first ignored, leading to defeat at Granicus in 334BC, and then followed only half-heartedly by local satraps reluctant to devastate their provinces to deny the Macedonians food. The long defence of Halicarnassus and successful counter-attacks in the eastern Aegean were part of Memnon's policy. But Memnon died in June 333BC, and his death led to a complete change in Persian strategy that soon proved disastrous.

Above: The Cyrus Cylinder, possibly from the reign of Persia's first monarch, was found at Babylon. It proclaims Persian ideals at their highest: "I will respect the traditions, customs and religions of the nations of my empire and never let my governors and subordinates look down on or insult them as long as I shall live." Such tolerance underlay Persian imperial success.

Below: The Palace of 100 Columns, one of the palaces in Persepolis in which court conspiracies arose to hamper Persian efforts to resist the Macedonian invasion.

CROSSING TO ASIA
334BC

Above: The ruins of Troy, which Alexander visited in 334BC and refounded as Alexandria-Troas. The city thrived for centuries afterward as a polis. It was also an early tourist site.

Early in May 334BC Alexander said goodbye to his mother, who reputedly told him the 'secret' of his birth. They never met again. Then he turned his back on his homeland and marched his army through Thrace to the Hellespont. There the remnants of Parmenion's advance force were waiting – they had been driven out of Asia – and the 160 ships mostly supplied by reluctant allies.

The Straits, only 4.5km/3 miles wide, had nasty currents, but the Macedonians were more worried about the threat of a Persian fleet, superior in size and skill. None appeared, however, either because a short-lived revolt in Egypt two years before still required its presence or, more probably, due to general indecisiveness and lack of preparation on the Persian side.

SACRIFICE AND LIBATIONS
Taking the helm of the royal trireme himself, Alexander led 60 ships across the Straits, the remainder taking a different route with Parmenion. Halfway across, he sacrificed a bull to Poseidon the sea god and poured out libations to the Nereids, sea nymphs. Alexander was always meticulous about observing such rites. He then changed into full armour. As the galley grounded on the Asian shore, he hurled his spear into Persian soil, symbolically claiming it as his, and leapt ashore, the first of the Macedonians. The landing, like the crossing, went unopposed, indeed probably unremarked, by the Persians, who were slowly assembling an army inland at Dascylium.

THE TOMB OF ACHILLES
The landscape around the Macedonian army was redolent with legend and myths. It was here, according to Homer, that the Achaeans had landed almost 1,000 years before to start their ten-year siege of Troy to win back Helen, the abducted queen of Sparta. Alexander felt he was literally treading in the steps of his hero Achilles. Now was the time and place to honour him

The splendid Troy of the 'topless towers' had long decayed to a mere village when Alexander approached it. His helmsman Menoitus crowned him with a golden laurel as he entered. Then, stripping

Left: Alexander shown between Hercules (on the right), a semi-divine hero with whom he was increasingly to identify, and Poseidon, the god of the sea, whom he was always careful to propitiate with due sacrifice.

THE PROBLEM OF SOURCES

Alexander used to lament that there was no Homer then living to immortalize him like Achilles in *The Iliad*. But he took with him an official historian: Callisthenes, a relative of Aristotle. Callisthenes boasted that he would make Alexander immortal, and at first depicted him sycophantically. But Callisthenes was executed in 327BC for conspiring against the king and his history has not survived. Nor has that of three other eye-witnesses: Ptolemy, Nearchus and Onesicritus.

Ptolemy, a boyhood friend of Alexander, became one of his generals and later founded the Ptolemaic kingdom of Egypt. He wrote knowledgeably but portrayed himself favourably while depicting rivals such as Perdiccas negatively. Nearchus, another boyhood friend, who commanded a fleet, lost all influence after Alexander's death. He wrote mostly on India and his voyages. Onesicritus was a philosopher who rather magnificently

tried to portray Alexander as a philosopher in arms. This required radical factual distortion. All three men's histories are lost. So too is that of Aristobulus, another eye-witness. An architect to Alexander, he compiled his history only when he was in his eighties.

Many later historians wrote about Alexander, one of the best being Quintus Curtius Rufus, a Roman of the 1st century AD. Plutarch and Arrian both wrote in the 2nd century AD under the Romans, and their biographies survive. Plutarch coupled Alexander with Julius Caesar in his *Parallel Lives*, which slanted his whole account. Arrian, who had been both a consul in Rome and a general, based his often excellent history, the best ancient account available, on Ptolemy and Nearchus. He presented a generally favourable yet not rose-tinted view of Alexander, but he was writing more than 400 years later.

Above: A coin of 323BC showing the goddess Athena from Sicyon, a Greek city in the League of Corinth, the last year of Alexander's reign.

Below: Achilles bandaging a wounded Patroclus, a scene inspired by (but not actually in) The Iliad. Alexander saw himself as a reincarnation of Achilles, the supreme hero, casting Hephaistion as a second Patroclus.

naked, he raced with his companions to the tomb of Achilles, placing a garland on it. Hephaistion ran similarly to the tomb of Patroclus. This was a very public declaration of their relationship.

At the altar of Zeus, Alexander prayed to Priam, legendary king of Troy, not to be angry with him as a descendant of Achilles, the Greek who had slain his son. Then he sacrificed at the temple of Athena, dedicating his suit of armour to the goddess. In return, he took from the temple a shield and weapons reputedly dating from the Trojan War. This set would accompany him across Asia as far as India. (Alexander, who always slept with a copy of *The Iliad* under his pillow, would face far greater challenges than his hero Achilles, however.) He granted Troy a new democratic constitution, renaming it Alexandria-Troas, under which name it flourished in subsequent centuries. Alexander then turned inland to meet and fight for the first time Persian forces.

CHAPTER III

THE GREAT VICTORIES

334–330BC

Alexander first faced the Persian army at the Granicus in May 334BC as an unknown young general confronting a mighty empire. Three and a half years later, after he had routed the grand Persian army on open plains in the empire's heart, he was being hailed as the new lord of Asia. Alexander had won three of the most important battles in history, two of them against far larger armies. In between he had captured the island city of Tyre, long thought invincible, after one of the hardest sieges ever undertaken. All these events show his strategic vision and tactical genius. Many Persian satraps and generals now began going over to his side, accepting the new reality of power, just as he began accepting Persian noblemen as administrators of his new-gained empire.

In between these battles came one of the most mysterious episodes in the life of any world conqueror: Alexander's pilgrimage to the shrine of the Egyptian god Ammon deep in the Libyan desert. What he learned there, in the sanctuary of the deity whom the Greeks identified with Zeus, remains unknown, but it seems to have spurred him to yet further efforts. In Egypt he also founded the city of Alexandria at the mouth of the Nile, an action that in itself would have made his name immortal. If he was indeed the son of a god, as he now began proclaiming on his coins and in his speeches,

Left: The Battle of Gaugamela, Alexander's crowning victory, depicted by the Renaissance artist Albrecht Altdorfer.

VICTORY AT GRANICUS
334 BC

Above: Alexander, filled with battle lust, leading his cavalry at Granicus, a sculpture attributed to Lysippus.

Below: The Persians had taken up a defensive position above the steep slopes of the river Granicus, for some reason placing their own cavalry in front of their Greek mercenary infantry. Alexander led his right wing further out before crossing the river to attack the Persian cavalry's flank, leaving his infantry to wade across the river downstream.

The Persians had failed to prevent the Macedonian army from crossing into Asia, probably because their fleet sent to repress an Egyptian rising a year earlier had not yet returned. However, they knew of the long-planned invasion, and the slowness of their reactions came from divisions in the regional high command.

MILITARY DIVISIONS
The generals in charge of the Persian army included Memnon, a Greek general from Rhodes, and Arsites, satrap of coastal Phrygia. While Memnon was no casual *condottiere* (leader of mercenaries) – he had been 15 years in Persian service, married a Persian wife and driven the Macedonians out of Asia the year before – he was no Persian aristocrat either, unlike the other generals. Many Persians had owned large estates in the area for generations. Perhaps for this reason his advice that they should retreat, laying waste the land and luring Alexander deep into Asia Minor while threatening his communications, was rejected by the other generals. Besides, Alexander, despite recent victories in the Balkans and at

Thebes, was still little known as a commander. There was no reason as yet to think him invincible.

PREPARING FOR ATTACK
So, gathering their forces, the Persian commanders decided to confront the invaders. Their troops were mostly local levies, although they included heavy armoured cavalry from Cappadocia in central Anatolia, making some 15,000 horsemen in all, plus *c*.20,000 Greek infantry. The Persians, who were not crack troops, were for once outnumbered by the Macedonians, whose forces totalled *c*.50,000. The Persians therefore needed a good position to offer a fight. They found one on the River Granicus, a small but swift river with steep banks.

Alexander's army encountered the Persians one May afternoon, unusually late in the day to start a battle. Parmenion, Philip's old general, reputedly advised waiting until dawn to attack, but Alexander replied that he would be ashamed if, after crossing the Hellespont, he let a mere stream delay him. He decided to launch a sudden attack before the Persians were fully prepared. (Or so wrote Arrian, our most reliable source.) Whatever the timing, Parmenion commanded the left wing while Alexander took the right, leading the Companion cavalry, his best troops.

ALEXANDER'S TACTIC
Plunging into the Granicus with his squadrons further upstream than expected, Alexander led his troops across obliquely, forcing the Persians to make a rapid adjustment. In Plutarch's words, Alexander "advanced through a hail of missiles towards a steep, well-defended bank, fighting the current that swept his men off their feet. His leadership seemed rash but he persisted... and reached the

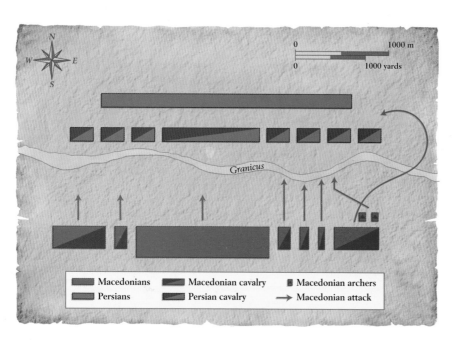

Macedonians

Persians

Macedonian cavalry

Persian cavalry

Macedonian archers

Macedonian attack

Left: Alexander's conquests took him from central Greece right across Asia to northern India, regions earlier known to Greeks only through legends and hearsay. As he marched east, he founded numerous cities to safeguard his conquests. Many have since prospered.

wet, muddy opposite bank, where he was forced to fight at once, man to man, before his supporting troops could get into formation... The Persians charged with a roar... closing in on Alexander whose shield and white-plumed helmet they recognized... the Persian generals Rhoseaces and Spithridates attacked him together." Alexander, almost killed when Spithridates split his helmet with an axe, was saved only by Cleitus 'the Black', who speared the Persian. On such timely intervention hung the whole fate of Asia.

The Macedonian cavalry, their long cornel-wood spears outreaching their opponents' lances, soon worsted the Persian cavalry. Seeing their generals killed, they turned and fled, leaving *c.*1,000 dead. The Greek mercenaries, who had been kept uselessly in the rear, now tried to make a stand. But, outnumbered and surrounded, they soon surrendered, although they managed to wound Alexander's horse.

AFTER THE BATTLE

"[Given by] Alexander, son of Philip, and the Greeks except for the Spartans, [taken] from the barbarians who live in Asia." With these words Alexander dedicated 300 suits of Persian armour taken from the defeated Persians to the goddess Athena on the Athenian Acropolis – significantly, the same number as the 300 Spartans who had fallen gallantly fighting Persia at Thermopylae in 480BC. This was brilliant propaganda. It ignored the fact that Granicus was overwhelmingly a *Macedonian* victory, stressing the tiny part played by Greeks on Alexander's side. Equally brilliant was the emphasis on the Spartans, who alone among the Greeks were not enrolled as Panhellenic allies (however reluctant) in the League of Corinth. Less clever was Alexander's treatment of the captured Greek mercenaries. He treated them all as traitors to the Panhellenic cause, killing many and sending 2,000 back to labour as slaves in Macedonia. This helped Macedonia's economy but, when other Greek mercenaries heard of it, they naturally chose to fight on rather than surrender.

Alexander visited the wounded Macedonians, recognizing many by name and praising their deeds. For the 25 Companions killed fighting, he decreed a hero's reward: Lysippus, the court sculptor, made statues of each and their families were exempted from taxation.

Below: Alexander crossing the Granicus as seen by the 17th-century artist Charles Lebrun. He was nearly killed in this, his first battle against Persia.

LIBERATING IONIA
334–333BC

Above: Miletus, one of the most defensible and important Ionian cities, was surrendered to Alexander by its garrison after only a short fight.

Below: Sardis, Persia's regional capital, was handed over to Alexander by its Persian governor without a blow but with its treasury. This combination earned the adaptable Persian a post on Alexander's staff.

After Granicus, Alexander forbade his men to plunder and marched upcountry to Sardis, the Lydian capital. The Persian commander surrendered, handing over its treasure and gaining a place on the Macedonian staff. Alexander promised to restore Lydia's old customs but made a brother of Parmenion its governor. His real concern was with the coastal Greek cities, whose liberation was among his avowed objectives.

THE RETURN OF DEMOCRACY
The cities of Ionia, some of the proudest in the Greek world, had been under Persian rule directly or indirectly since the King's Peace of 386BC. Persia had normally favoured oligarchies, finding them easier to deal with than democracies, but the result was growing political tensions between rich and poor inside these cities. This discontent erupted on the news of Alexander's victory. At Ephesus, one of the largest cities, a pro-Persian junta was expelled. Alexander restored the exiled democrats, who began taking bloody revenge until he forbade it. Other cities now welcomed him, as he "broke up oligarchies everywhere, men being given their own laws and exempted from the tribute they had paid the barbarians [Persians]". Instead Alexander, with forceful tact, asked for *syntaxeis* (contributions) to his war chest.

While Alexander favoured democracy in Ionia for essentially pragmatic reasons, elsewhere preferring other forms of government, his actions marked a true liberation, long remembered with gratitude by the cities concerned. Fifty years later, a decree from the little city of Priene, rebuilt on his orders, proclaimed: "There is no greater blessing for Greeks than freedom." Whether Greek cities on the Asian mainland were incorporated into the League of Corinth remains debatable. The non-Hellenic countryside around certainly remained unfree, with Macedonia simply replacing Persia as its feudal overlord.

SURRENDER AT MILETUS
At Miletus, strongly defended on its headland, the garrison resisted, encouraged by the large Persian fleet now nearby. Refusing to fight at sea, Alexander moved rapidly to the assault, battering his way into the city with his siege engines. The garrison, who had swum out to a tiny island, happily accepted Alexander's offer of clemency, 300 enlisting in his army.

Alexander then unexpectedly disbanded his fleet, saying he would conquer the sea by land, in other words capture the Persians' bases in Asia. In truth, he could not afford to pay 160 triremes' inactive crews of 32,000 men. He kept only 20 Athenian ships, whose crews served as hostages for their city.

SIEGE OF HALICARNASSUS

On the southern edge of Ionia lay Halicarnassus, a half-Greek, half-Carian city, its massive walls rising in a semicircle with a sea-girt citadel. Memnon, now commander of lower Asia and the whole fleet, was there with many Greek mercenaries. Alexander, marching toward it through the forests inland, was approached by Ada, widowed queen of Caria, into whose family he had tried to marry three years before. No longer a nervous adolescent but an assured king, he welcomed her surrender, reappointing her as queen with a Macedonian commander. He then became her adopted son, so winning over the Carians. (What Olympias back home thought of this is unrecorded.) But to take Halicarnassus required force.

After early skirmishing and an unsuccessful attempt to take a nearby port by surprise, the Macedonians filled in many of the city's ditches. They now turned their catapults against its walls, knocking them down in parts. But the garrison, sallying out at night, torched many of these wooden engines. Some Macedonian soldiers, getting drunk, then launched an impromptu attack on the city that ended disastrously. Memnon personally led the defenders out to repulse them. Another sortie three days later panicked the Macedonians until Alexander himself led a counter-charge, driving the defenders back. The city, shutting its gates prematurely, lost many troops and Memnon ordered a retreat to the castle. He soon sailed away, although the castle held out for a year. The two-month siege had been won more by force than great generalship.

CUTTING THE GORDIAN KNOT

It was now autumn, normally a time for rest and recuperation, but these were not concepts that Alexander recognized. Giving all recently married troops winter leave (a popular measure that also boosted the birth-rate), he entered Lycia and Pamphylia, whose steep coastlines were dotted with small Greek cities.

Capturing these in his role of Panhellenic liberator – Aspendos, one of the chief cities, betrayed him and was severely fined – he turned north. Uniting with the troops back from Macedonia, he entered central Anatolia.

At Gordium he saw the Gordian Knot in the old palace of golden King Midas. Whoever untied it, said the legend, would control Asia. After fiddling fruitlessly, Alexander drew his sword and cut through it, in a way fulfilling the prophecy. But as he marched east that summer of 333BC, he left Memnon with a large fleet still threatening his rear.

Above: The lion of Didyma, one of the many Ionian cities that flourished again after Alexander's conquest, which was for them a true liberation.

Below: The Temple of Athena Polias at Priene, an Ionian city rebuilt with Alexander's help to become almost the perfect polis. Alexander's restoration of Priene as a democracy was long remembered with gratitude.

AN UNEXPECTED BATTLE: ISSUS 333BC

Above: Darius III, the last Achaemenid king, in growing terror as he spots Alexander hurtling towards him.

Below: At Issus, Persian numerical superiority was annulled by the narrowness of the site. Alexander thinned his centre and led his cavalry on the right in an oblique attack that crumpled up the Persian centre where Darius was.

As Alexander approached the Cilician Gates, an easily defended pass through the Taurus Mountains, the Persians abandoned it. They had burnt their fields, either following Memnon's scorched-earth policy or just panicking, so the Macedonians entered Cilicia unopposed. There Alexander fell gravely ill after bathing in a river. Warned by letter that his Greek physician Philip was trying to poison him, Alexander showed Philip the letter, took his medicine – and recovered. But he had lost two months lying ill.

DARIUS'S NEW STRATEGY

The general situation, meanwhile, had changed completely. Memnon, the Persians' general, died in June 333BC on campaign in the Aegean. This bad news led Darius to rethink his strategy. Deciding to go to war in person, he began massing armies, moving to Babylon. Persia had abundant cavalry even without horsemen from its further satrapies, but lacked heavy infantry apart from the 10,000

Immortals and some youthful trainees. So Darius recalled the 15,000 Greek hoplites fighting under Memnon's successors. When Persian forces left Babylon in September, they totalled *c.*150,000, far more than the Macedonians. But most had little or no military experience.

By late September, Alexander had recovered. Unaware of recent events, he decided to continue capturing Persia's naval supply ports. Parmenion went ahead to seize the Syrian Gates, the pass through the Amanus mountains, while Alexander hunted and waited on events in the Aegean. Then came startling news: the main Persian army was camped beyond the Amanus range. Alexander raced east with his army.

Leaving the sick at Issus in the corner of the gulf, he continued south down the coast, hoping to catch the Persians in the rear. But Darius, growing anxious, decided to seek out Alexander. He moved north behind the Amanus while Alexander, unaware, marched south on the coast. When the Persians crossed the Amanus, they had cut Alexander off. The Persians mutilated the Macedonian invalids they found at Issus, although some escaped to warn Alexander. He seemed trapped with no escape route.

BATTLE BY THE SHORE

Alexander, swinging around, marched his weary men back through the night until the two armies faced each other between the sea and mountains. As usual, he commanded the Companion cavalry on the right, Parmenion taking the left. Darius sent light troops up into the mountains. Alexander countered by sending archers to drive them back. He then reinforced his left wing by the coast but thinned his centre. Darius was in the Persian centre with his Greek mercenaries. Between them lay the stream of the Pinarus,

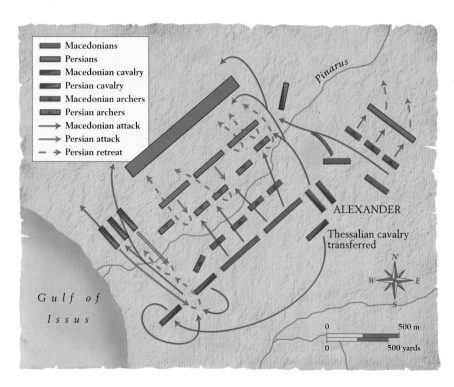

Macedonians
Persians
Macedonian cavalry
Persian cavalry
Macedonian archers
Persian archers
→ Macedonian attack
→ Persian attack
--→ Persian retreat

Pinarus

ALEXANDER

Thessalian cavalry transferred

Gulf of Issus

0   500 m
0   500 yards

swollen by autumn floods. At noon on 1 November 333BC, Alexander gave the signal to attack.

The Macedonian cavalry surged forward, crossing the river. The infantry followed more slowly, raising their fearful war cry "ALALALAI!" The two armies met head on. Macedonian cavalry at once broke through the Persian line. Then Alexander wheeled his horsemen obliquely in toward the centre, rolling up the Persian riders on their flanks in a brilliant manoeuvre. He was heading for Darius, very visible in his chariot. Parmenion repulsed the Persian cavalry but in the centre Persia's Greek mercenaries threatened the exposed phalanx until Alexander's advance forced them to retreat. Darius, seeing Alexander cutting relentlessly toward him, turned his chariot and fled. Swapping his chariot for a horse, he abandoned even his royal cloak. Alexander pursued him until night fell, then turned back. Victory was his, won by audacious cavalry tactics.

AFTER THE BATTLE

The Persians had suffered heavily, although the traditionally cited figure of 110,000 dead is incredible. The Macedonians had 4,500 wounded and many hundreds dead. Hearing women crying nearby, Alexander discovered they were Darius' womenfolk, mourning a king they believed dead. He sent reassurances,

ordering that they should be treated as royalty. Next day at their meeting, the Persian queen mother did obeisance to the taller Hephaistion. Realizing her error, she was mortified until Alexander said: "You make no mistake, madame, he too is Alexander."

He also met Barsine again, whom he had known long ago in Pella. She now became his mistress and bore him a son, forming a useful link between east and west. He then visited the wounded Macedonians, congratulating each man he had seen in battle and arranging a magnificent funeral for the dead. On the battle site he founded a city: Alexandria, today Alexandretta.

Above: After the battle, Alexander went with Hephaistion to comfort Darius' women, mourning a king they assumed dead. The queen mother saluted Hephaistion as Alexander, a mistake Alexander courteously shrugged off. This is the Renaissance artist Veronese's grand depiction of the scene.

Below: The Battle of Issus was primarily a cavalry action, which is how Jan Brueghel painted it in this dramatic canvas of 1602.

THE SPOILS OF VICTORY

Alexander was astonished by the luxury of the Persian royal tents. Even on campaign, Darius travelled in style: "When he [Alexander] saw the gold bowls, pitchers and tubs, exquisitely worked and set in a chamber fragrant with incense and spices, when he entered a tent of remarkable size and height, set with sofas and tables for his dinner, he looked at his Companions and remarked: 'This, it seems, is what it is to be king.'"

THE SIEGE OF TYRE
332BC

Above: The siege of Tyre in 332BC, as imagined in a medieval miniature.

Dispatching Parmenion to Damascus to seize the Persian war chest of 2,600 talents there, Alexander turned south to the cities of Phoenicia. Along with Cyprus, Phoenicia supplied the Persians with their fleet, although it had little love for the empire. Sidon, where a revolt had been brutally suppressed 12 years before, welcomed Alexander, as did Byblos. Tyre, the most powerful Phoenician city, invited Alexander to sacrifice to Hercules, its patron god, in old Tyre on the mainland, but refused to let Macedonians – or Persians – into the island city. Alexander, who could not leave a great naval power neutral behind him (as he told his army) decided to capture it. This was easier proclaimed than done.

CONSTRUCTING A MOLE
Tyre, a walled island 4.8km/3 miles in circumference, was reputedly impregnable, having once withstood a siege by a Babylonian king for 13 years. It lay

Below: A battle scene between Macedonians and Persians from the Sidon Sarcophagus. *Sidon, Tyre's neighbour and rival, supported Alexander.*

800m/880 yards from the mainland in sea that was 180m/600ft deep. On the land side its thick walls rose to 45m/150ft and it had a powerful fleet. Alexander had no fleet at all and his torsion catapults had a maximum range of only 270m/300 yards. Yet in January 332BC he began to build a mole, or causeway, out of the ruins of old Tyre to let his catapults and siege towers reach the city. So started the seven-month siege, the greatest in antiquity.

At first all went well, but as the mole entered deeper waters, it came within range of Tyrian catapults, while triremes sallied from the city's twin harbours to rain arrows on the workers. Alexander ordered in siege towers as protection. In response, the Tyrians secretly built a vast fireship. When a favourable wind blew, they sailed this floating bomb across the waters. On impact, it was ignited, torching the mole's towers and catapults. Undaunted, Alexander ordered the mole rebuilt, only this time wider to take more

engines and towers. Then he went north to friendly Sidon, where he had some very good news.

The fleets of Sidon and neighbouring cities had returned, deserting the Persian side. With their 100 ships, plus 120 from Cyprus and 9 from Rhodes, Alexander now had supremacy at sea. Attempts to lure Tyre's fleet out failed, however, for the Tyrians blocked their harbours. Instead, the other Phoenicians built floating battering rams protected by roofs of fireproof hide. They rowed these around to attack Tyre's weaker seaward walls.

Meanwhile, Alexander's engineers rebuilt the mole wider and at an angle to the prevailing wind. On to it rolled the tallest siege towers yet seen: 20 storeys high with battering rams and catapults on their upper decks. Soon Tyre was besieged on all sides.

LONG RESISTANCE OF TYRE

But the Tyrians were not defeated yet. Hanging leather skins stuffed with seaweed from their battlements, they cushioned their walls against missiles. They dropped rocks on to siege ships and sent underwater divers to cut the Macedonian vessels' moorage cables, after which the Macedonians switched to solid chain. Then the Tyrians used sharp poles to slice through the ropes holding the battering rams and poured red-hot sand on to the besiegers below, penetrating the attackers' armour and causing them agony. By late June, as stalemate threatened, some advised a truce; Tyre was no longer so vital since other fleets had become allies. A letter came from Darius, offering all land west of the Euphrates, his daughter in marriage and 10,000 talents. Reputedly, Parmenion urged acceptance but Alexander refused. He wanted the whole empire – and he would not leave Tyre untaken.

THE FINAL ONSLAUGHT

One hot July noon, when the besiegers were lunching or snoozing, Tyre's best ships slipped out and attacked the

Cypriot fleet, sinking five galleys. Alexander broke off his lunch to lead the counter-attack, sinking all the Tyrians. By now Tyre was both starving and without allies. Alexander began an all-out attack on every side of the city at once. The fleets attacked the seaward walls and both harbours while siege towers and catapults assaulted the land side from the mole. Overwhelmed, the Tyrian defences collapsed and the Macedonians poured into the city early in August. Alexander had conquered the sea from the land.

Alexander killed 8,000 Tyrians, crucifying 2,000. The rest were sold into slavery, the customary fate. Tyre gained a Greek name and constitution but never regained its primacy. As Alexander advanced toward Egypt, only Gaza, the old Philistine stronghold, refused to surrender. Its siege took two long months, during which Alexander was twice wounded. When Gaza finally fell, Alexander dragged its commander, Batis, around the walls behind his chariot – an excruciating death. (Achilles in *The Iliad* had similarly dragged Hector around Troy, but the Trojan prince was already dead. This was gratuitous cruelty.)

Above: Totally destroying the old Phoenician city of Tyre, Alexander refounded it as a Greek city. It thrived under the Roman empire, as Roman-era ruins attest.

Below: Tyre, on its massively fortified island, was thought impregnable. Alexander proved otherwise, but it took him seven months and tested his military genius to its limits.

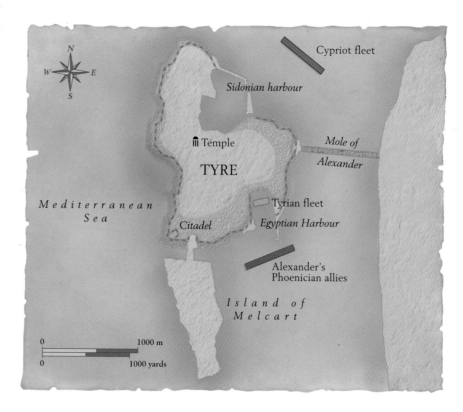

EGYPT: THE FOUNDING OF ALEXANDRIA 332–331 BC

Above: Alexander, crowned as Pharaoh by Egyptian priests, was depicted on temple carvings as being greeted by Ammon Ra, greatest god of the Egyptian pantheon.

Below: A 19th-century view of the great harbour at Alexandria showing all that remains of the lighthouse, once one of the Seven Wonders of the World. For 1,000 years after its foundation in 331 BC, Alexandria was one of the greatest cities on earth.

Egypt had known, and generally accepted, the Greeks as traders, mercenaries and colonists (at Naucratis in the Delta) for more than two centuries. It had even seen some of the very first tourists, such as Herodotus, that insatiably curious historian-traveller of the 5th century BC.

PERSIAN MISRULE

The country had been in intermittent revolt against Persia for 130 years, remaining independent for more than 60 years of the 4th century BC. (Its customs and religion, which intrigued the Greeks, seem to have annoyed the Zoroastrian Persians, who were essentially monotheistic.) Persian behaviour had been at best insensitive, at worst deliberately offensive, to Egypt's powerful priesthood and the devout *fellahin* (peasantry), who made up the bulk of this strongly hierarchical society.

"In Egypt," Plato had observed, "it is impossible for a king to rule without the priests." Persian soldiers had reputedly roasted and eaten the sacred bull Apis, replacing it with a donkey – an animal the Egyptians loathed. But despite this, many Egyptian temples had retained their estates under Persian rule.

When Alexander crossed the desert in late 332 BC, the Persian governor of the frontier fort of Pelusium opened its gates to him. Alexander then sailed up the Nile to Memphis unopposed. In the ancient capital he was enthusiastically welcomed by the people and priests and lodged in the old palace of the pharaohs. Alexander sacrificed to the Egyptian gods, especially Apis, and was crowned Pharaoh, as inscriptions in the temples attest. As Pharaoh, he was the son of Horus, the divine son of the sun god Ra, and also beloved son of Ammon, creator of the Universe. These titles impressed him far more deeply than his Companions probably at first suspected.

CHOOSING THE SITE

Alexander held athletic games "to which the most famous performers came from all over Greece", according to Arrian, then sailed down the west branch of the Nile and around Lake Mareotis to the sea. Here he was struck by "the excellence of the site, convinced that if a city were built upon it, it would prosper. Filled with enthusiasm, he himself oversaw the layout of the new city, indicating the site for the

THE ROSETTA STONE

Much of what we know about ancient Egypt under the ancient Pharaohs and the Ptolemies derives from the Rosetta Stone, a trilingual slab dating from 196BC. In that year Ptolemy V (descended from Alexander's general Ptolemy I) set up the stone bearing a declaration in three languages: Greek (the language spoken in Alexandria and in government); demotic Egyptian (spoken by native Egyptians); and hieroglyphs (the ancient sign-writing read only by priests). Ptolemy V's government, facing problems after military defeats and peasant revolts, put up trilingual stones proclaiming that Ptolemy was the truly anointed Pharaoh. This stone was found in the city of Rosetta – hence its name – during the French occupation of Egypt under Napoleon in 1799. It was taken to London after the British expelled the French. The French had made copies of the writing and after 1815 a race developed between the two countries to decipher the stone first. The brilliant French Egyptologist François Champollion finally cracked the hieroglyphs in 1822–4.

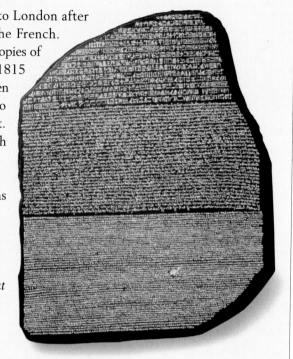

Right: The stone found at Rosetta contained trilingual inscriptions that enabled the Egyptologist Champollion finally to decipher it in 1824.

market square and the temples, Greek gods being chosen along with the Egyptian Isis, and the exact limits of its walls." (Arrian again.) Alexander sprinkled barley meal taken from his soldiers' rucksacks to mark out the city's walls – an omen that Aristander, his prophet, interpreted to mean that the city would enjoy the fruits of the earth.

GREATEST MEDITERRANEAN CITY

There had long been a trading post on the offshore island of Pharos, on which, according to a legend, the lovers Helen and Paris of Troy had hidden after fleeing Sparta. Sheltering the harbour from the prevailing north winds that kept the site cool in summer, Pharos became famous for the giant lighthouse on it. Alexandria itself soon became the greatest city in the Mediterranean, a trading metropolis renowned for luxury and culture, with the biggest library in the world.

Alexander could not have foreseen all this, but he certainly envisaged the city as Egypt's new capital, well sited to receive the grain and other products flowing down the Nile, while looking out toward Greece. Alexander settled Macedonian veterans, Greeks, prisoners and some Jews in his new city. Later, under the Ptolemies and Romans, Alexandria seems to have lacked a council and assembly, but its founder may have originally granted it these vital aspects of a Greek *polis*. Alexandria-in-Egypt, despite many vicissitudes, would flourish until the Arab conquest nearly a thousand years later.

Below: Sailing unopposed up the Nile to the ancient capital Memphis, Alexander was welcomed by the Egyptians, who had come to loathe the Persians.

EGYPT: THE PILGRIMAGE TO SIWAH 331BC

Above: The Temple of Horus at Edfu was built under the Ptolemies, the Hellenistic kings who succeeded Alexander. It is the best preserved of all Egyptian temples.

Below: The Temple of Ammon at Siwah, the mysterious oasis-shrine that Alexander visited in 331BC.

The most mysterious episode in Alexander's life may have originated in a simple desire to explore the vague western frontier of Egypt, his newest conquest. Early in 331BC he led a small group west along the coast from the Nile. Then he turned due south into the desert, heading for Siwah, an oasis 320km/200 miles inland with a famous shrine. Siwah had long been revered by the citizens of Cyrene, the greatest Greek city in Libya. Cyrenians worshipped its ram-headed god Ammon/Amun as Zeus. (The Greeks, being tolerant polytheists, often identified other people's deities with their own.) Through Cyrene's influence, Siwah's fame had spread to Greece proper, where it was seen as an African version of the Delphic oracle. But Siwah itself, although visited by a few Greeks remained mysterious.

UNKNOWN MOTIVES

Alexander's true motives for this long diversion, while Darius was slowly assembling Persia's Grand Army beyond the Euphrates, remain disputed. For some people his desert pilgrimage reveals his mystical belief in his destiny; others view it as an attempt to bolster his position with his new subjects, Egyptian and others. Callisthenes, the official historian, said that it was due to Alexander's "thirst for glory and because he heard Hercules and Perseus had gone there before him". These were heroes Alexander always strove to rival.

HOLY GUIDES

Riding camels, the party left the coast at Paraetonium, entering a sand desert. After four days' wandering, they had almost run out of water when a rainstorm enabled them to refill their water bottles.

From then on they travelled by night to avoid the heat through a landscape later described by the Victorian traveller Bayle St John: "A gorge black as Erebus lies across the path and on the right stands a huge pile of rocks, looking like the ruins of some vast fabulous city.... There were yawning gateways flanked by bastions of immense altitude; there were towers and pyramids and crescents and domes and dizzy pinnacles and majestic crenellated heights, all invested with unearthly grandeur by the magic light of the moon."

Unsurprisingly, Alexander's party became lost, until (according to Ptolemy) two holy serpents appeared to guide them through the Pass of the Crow and down to the first oasis. Beyond a glittering white salt desert lay Siwah itself, green and lush with palm and fruit trees.

THE ORACLE'S ANSWER

The chief priest emerged from the temple to invite Alexander into the sanctuary, not requiring him to change his travel-stained clothes, like most supplicants. The other Macedonians, left in an outer courtyard,

can have heard little of what went on in the temple's dim recesses, but Callisthenes recorded it as if he had: "The oracles were not given in spoken words as at Delphi or Miletus, but mostly given in nods and signs, just as in Homer '[Zeus] spoke and nodded assent with his dark brows.' The prophet answered for Zeus, telling the king directly that he was the son of Zeus." All Alexander would say afterwards was that he was pleased with the result.

Returning without trouble to Memphis, he divided Egypt's government between civilian and soldiers, a sensible arrangement he later repeated elsewhere. Then he moved north, gathering his armies at Tyre for the decisive encounter with Darius' Grand Army.

Above: At the remote but famous sanctuary of Ammon, whom the Greeks identified with Zeus, Alexander was reputedly told that he was the son of Zeus, an answer that fully "satisfied him".

ALEXANDER THE GOD

"Zeus is the father of all men but makes the best especially his own," Alexander once said. For Greeks, there was no sharp division between gods and men, the world being filled with gods. The kings of both Sparta and Macedonia claimed descent from Hercules, the mythical hero who became a god. Lysander, the Spartan general who defeated Athens in 404BC, was hailed as a god by grateful oligarchs. Philip II was later portrayed like an Olympian deity on some coins and statues. After his Siwah pilgrimage, Alexander began invoking Zeus as his father, implying his own divinity. (He regarded Ammon as a form of universal Zeus, not a local deity.) This later caused problems. When Alexander first tried to get Macedonians to offer him *proskynesis* – the homage Persians paid their Great King, although monotheistic Persians never *worshipped* their monarch – he had to back down.

Finally, in 324BC Alexander, at the height of his powers, ordained his deification, which produced varying reactions. The Ionian cities, already worshipping Alexander, complied happily; the Spartans replied laconically: "Alexander can call himself a god if he wishes"; and Demosthenes probably spoke for most Athenians when he said, "Alexander can be the son of Zeus – and of Poseidon also if he wants." After his death, Alexander was often depicted as divine with the horns of Ammon, and many of his successors claimed godlike attributes.

Right: Alexander with the horns of Ammon, the Egyptian deity he claimed as his father, on a coin issued by Ptolemy I (ruled Egypt 323–284BC).

THE GREAT VICTORY: GAUGAMELA 331BC

Above: The archetypal image of Alexander at the charge, huge-eyed and with wind-swept hair.

Alexander waited in Tyre through the early summer until he heard that Darius had mustered the Persian Grand Army in Babylonia. He did not want another inconclusive battle like Issus but needed to defeat the Persians totally and openly. However, Darius was based in Babylon 1,120km/700 miles from the Mediterranean, far beyond Alexander's knowledge. In July, Hephaistion went north to the River Euphrates with an advance guard. He found himself facing Mazaeus, a Persian satrap of Syria, with 3,000 troops, mostly Greek mercenaries. For some weeks the two forces faced each other, perhaps exchanging secret messages. Then, as Alexander approached with his 47,000-strong army, Mazaeus retreated, burning the fertile Euphrates valley. Alexander took the northern unburnt route towards the Tigris – a fast-flowing river hard to cross if defended.

THE SITE OF THE BATTLE

Curiously, his army was unopposed as it crossed the river, the cavalry wading in upstream to shelter the infantry. The land around was invitingly unravaged. Darius probably was luring the Macedonians on to a spacious battlefield (the plain of Gaugamela) of his choosing. On 20 September the Moon eclipsed. Alexander sacrificed to the Sun, Moon and Earth, revealing astronomical knowledge learned from Aristotle and also Greek piety. Aristander, his prophet, interpreted the ominous event favourably. Then Alexander heard that Darius was camped nearby with a "force much larger than at Issus". Ignoring advice to try a night attack (always risky), Alexander rested his army while he reconnoitred. What he saw was awesomely impressive.

Darius had mustered the largest army that he could feed, perhaps 250,000 men. He meant to win by sheer numbers. Crucially, he had *c.*40,000 cavalry, while Alexander had only 7,000. Only in heavy infantry were the Persians weaker, deprived of Greek recruits. To let their chariots charge smoothly, the Persians had cleared the ground while fixing stakes to protect their flanks. Having seen the Persian set-up, Alexander planned at leisure, keeping the Persians waiting for two nights. At noon on 1 October 331BC the battle for Asia began.

THE OPPOSING ARMIES

On the Persian left was the formidable Bactrian and Scythian cavalry commanded by their satrap Bessus. Mazaeus commanded the cavalry on the right. In the centre was Darius, protected by 15 Indian elephants (whose smell panics horses that are unused to them), 6,000 Greek hoplites, the Persian infantry and

Above: Indo-Greek tetradrachms and staters struck by the kings of Bactria.

Below: The Azara Herm, a copy of an original by Lysippus, showing the dynamic conqueror in distinctly tough-looking mode. Alexander was always keenly aware of the propaganda value of his image.

200 scythed chariots. The Persians could potentially outflank the Macedonians on both sides.

Alexander slanted his whole army obliquely, with 10,000 sarissa-wielding heavy infantry in the centre. Their right flank was protected by 3,000 mobile Shield Bearers, linked to the Companion cavalry on the right led by Alexander himself. Ahead of them ran 2,000 archers, slingers and javelin throwers. On the left wing, under Parmenion, were the Thessalian horsemen and remaining Macedonian cavalry, forming the anchor of the slanting line. Alexander's wing actually found itself opposite Darius' centre. To counter flank attacks, Alexander ordered the infantry to face about if needed to form a square – a manoeuvre requiring perfect discipline. At the tip of each cavalry wing, infantry units of veteran mercenaries were concealed, a tactic first recommended by Xenophon.

Alexander began battle by leading his wing to the right while holding back Parmenion's troops. This drew the Persian left flank out, away from their elephants and defences. The Bactrians charged, trying to outflank the Macedonians, but the latter's cavalry wedges turned to face them, foot soldiers emerging to drive back the disconcerted Bactrians. In the centre the chariots were countered by archers. Any surviving chariots rattled harmlessly through infantry ranks that opened up.

THE FLIGHT OF THE KING

As Alexander intended, a gap appeared to the left of Darius' centre. Into it he led his Companion cavalry in a wedge-shaped attack heading for the Great King. The Shield Bearers followed on foot. Darius, again seeing nemesis on a black horse bearing down, again turned and fled – Alexander reputedly got close enough to kill the royal charioteer. Meanwhile, the Persian cavalry under Mazaeus on the right beat back Parmenion's wing, pushing past into the Macedonian camp. There they discovered the Persian Queen Mother, who looked at them in stony,

immobile silence until they withdrew. Other gaps appeared in the central Macedonian line but the troops turned to form oblongs. Then news of the Great King's flight demoralized the Persian army. Mazaeus, recalling his unbeaten cavalry, rode hard for Babylon.

The battle had been won by just 3,000 cavalry Companions supported by 8,000 Shield Bearers under Alexander's visionary leadership. He tried to pursue Darius, but swirling masses of retreating troops, thick clouds of dust and then nightfall hampered him. Darius swapped his chariot for a horse and rode into the mountains of Media. On the battlefield Alexander was hailed as lord of Asia.

Above: The Battle of Gaugamela, *as painted by the French 17th-century artist Lebrun. Macedonian victory at this huge battle determined the fate of half Asia.*

Below: Heavily outnumbered at Gaugamela, Alexander slanted his army obliquely so that the right wing, under his command, attacked the Persian centre. Alexander's wedge-shaped cavalry formations cut through the Persian ranks and Darius fled in contagious panic.

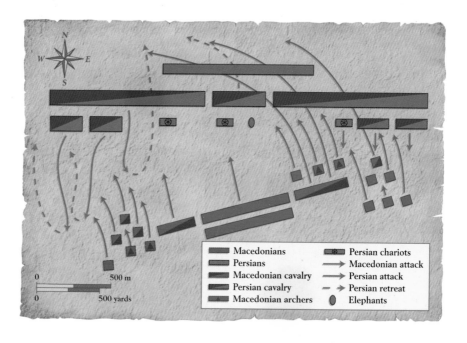

Macedonians		Persian chariots
Persians		Macedonian attack
Macedonian cavalry		Persian attack
Persian cavalry		Persian retreat
Macedonian archers		Elephants

0   500 m

0   500 yards

IN BABYLON
331BC

Above: The Babylonians offering Alexander the city's keys, from a French medieval painting.

Below: Alexander entered Babylon in triumph, its citizens welcoming him as a liberator from Persian misrule, depicted in an 18th-century painting by Gasparo Diziano.

When Alexander reached Arbela 112km/70 miles away, he realized that Darius had vanished into the mountains of Media (Kurdistan), at which point he abandoned the pursuit. After burying his dead (Persian casualties far outnumbered Macedonian, but even they had suffered heavily, Hephaistion being among the wounded), he quit the battlefield.

South lay Babylon, the greatest metropolis of Asia, "surpassing in splendour any city in the known world", as Herodotus had written 150 years earlier. Still a great trading city, Babylon was also an important religious centre. Its Chaldean priests were famed as mathematicians, astronomers and astrologers. Babylon's defences of brick-built walls were 60m/200ft high and wide enough for chariots to drive around two abreast, according to Herodotus. Surrounded by deep moats, they rivalled Tyre's.

ALEXANDER WELCOMED
But there was to be no siege of Babylon. As the Macedonians warily approached the city, its gates opened and the Persian general Mazaeus rode out with his sons to greet Alexander. Behind him came Babylonian priests chanting and dancing, with city magistrates bearing gifts to indicate their surrender. Alexander mounted a special chariot to ride in triumph up the dead straight avenues toward the royal palace, a complex with 600 rooms. This welcome from Babylon's elite was both politic and heart-felt.

PERSIAN MISRULE
Like Egypt, Babylon and Babylonia had often been maltreated by the Persians. While Cyrus, its first Persian ruler, had meticulously respected Babylon's customs and deities, later kings such as Xerxes had abused the city, demoting it from being the satrapy capital after a revolt and expropriating its temple treasures. Persian rule had drained Babylonia of wealth and even population (it had to send 500 eunuchs and 1,000 talents of silver to the Persian court each year). Many farms had been given to Persian nobles as estates, while the irrigation channels on which Babylonia's fertility relied were neglected.

THE HANGING GARDENS OF BABYLON

One of the Seven Wonders of the Ancient World, the Hanging Gardens of Babylon displayed Babylonian wealth and ingenuity. Traditionally they were built *c*.600BC for Amytis, the Median-born wife of King Nebuchadnezar II, homesick for her green native mountains. Babylon had many massive ziggurat temples and other buildings, often with walls 25m/80ft thick, mostly dating from that period.

Archaeologists have not yet decided which ruins in Babylon are the Gardens described by Greek writers such as Strabo and Diodorus Siculus in the 1st century BC. Diodorus wrote: "The approach to the Garden sloped like a steep hill and the several parts of the structure rose from one another tier on tier. On all this earth had been piled and was thickly planted with trees of every kind that, by their size and beauty, delighted beholders... Water machines raised abundant supplies of water from the river,

Left: The Hanging Gardens of Babylon, one of the Seven Wonders of the Ancient World, as imagined in a a 19th-century illustration.

though hidden from view." Clearly the Babylonians had pumps to raise water from the Euphrates, and they waterproofed their brickwork. Confusion comes from a translation error: the Greek word *kremastos* means *overhanging*, not hanging. Creepers and branches overhung the walls of this sky-garden.

Above: The Ishtar Gate, Babylon's grandest ceremonial gate, for which the city was renowned, was dedicated to Ishtar, the goddess of sacred prostitution.

TEMPLES AND BROTHELS

Concerned as ever to give the local gods their due, Alexander sacrificed in the temple of Bel-Marduk, Babylon's patron deity. He then clasped the hand of the golden statue to show that, like the old Babylonian kings, he received his power direct from the god. He took the old title King of the Lands and ordained the rebuilding of E-sagila, the great ziggurat-temple 60m/200ft high, damaged by Xerxes. He also ordered that Greek plants be added to the varieties growing luxuriantly in Babylon's famous Hanging Gardens, although few probably survived Babylon's heat. But he reappointed the Persian Mazaeus as satrap, with Apollodorus as Macedonian military governor – a wise balance repeated elsewhere later. Persians who knew the locality were obviously useful.

While Alexander was restoring the temples, his men were enjoying the city's equally famous brothels, helped by a

generous pay bonus. Quantities of gold, in ingots rather than coin, had been found in the city, which were minted into coins to pay the army. (Herodotus had noted the strange Babylonian custom that required *all* women to ritually prostitute themselves in temples before marriage.)

After a month's rest and recreation, the army marched out south-east towards Susa and Persepolis, the Persian capitals.

Below: Babylon's walls gleamed with enamelled bricks depicting animals such as this lion.

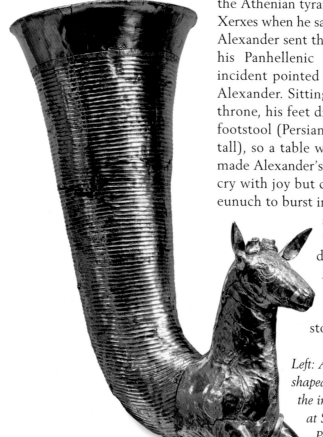

THE DESTRUCTION OF PERSEPOLIS 331–330BC

Susa, the eastern terminus of the Royal Road that ran west to Sardis, lay in the Elamite plain, not Persia proper. Although reputedly even hotter than Babylon, Darius I (522–486BC), the greatest Achaemenid king, had made it his growing empire's administrative capital. From Susa's huge palace, orders, threats and bribes had gone out to Greece for nearly 200 years, so its name sounded sinister to Greek or Macedonian ears. However, the army entered Susa unopposed.

WEALTH OF SUSA AND PERSEPOLIS
The Macedonians were stunned by the accumulated wealth of the Persian kings – 50,000 talents of silver, according to Arrian, plus rich carpets and furnishings. Among the treasures were the bronze statues of Harmodius and Aristogeiton, the Athenian tyrannicides carried off by Xerxes when he sacked Athens in 480BC. Alexander sent them home, reaffirming his Panhellenic credentials. Another incident pointed to new dilemmas for Alexander. Sitting on the Great King's throne, his feet did not reach the royal footstool (Persian kings were generally tall), so a table was fetched. The sight made Alexander's old friend Demaratus cry with joy but caused a Persian court eunuch to burst into tears. To reconcile such disparate groups would prove very difficult, but at present Alexander was still Panhellenic leader. Even more treasure was stored at Persepolis, the

Above: Two bull-headed columns among the ruins of the huge palace of Darius I in Persepolis, which Alexander burnt one drunken evening.

Left: A gold rhyton (animal-shaped drinking vessel), part of the immense treasures stored at Susa and especially at Persepolis, then considered the "richest city on earth."

ceremonial capital in Persia's mountainous heart. Sending Parmenion with the baggage by the slower road, in December Alexander took the direct route with the Companion cavalry and best troops. En route he crushed some tribesmen, accustomed to demanding tribute from passing Persians, by a dawn raid that shocked them into surrender and paying *him* tribute of 30,000 sheep a year. (They were shepherds, not farmers.) Finally he entered Iranian territory, unknown to the Greeks, and approached the Persian Gates.

THE PERSIAN GATES
The Gates were a formidable natural barrier of rock strengthened by walls, blocking a 2,150m/7,000ft high pass. Lining them were 40,000 troops, whose catapults showered boulders and arrows on the Macedonians. Mauled, the latter hastily retreated. For a moment Alexander seemed baffled. Then a shepherd told him of a rough path that ran high up behind the pass. Leaving some men with orders to attack when they heard trumpets, he took the others on a night march of 17km/11 miles through snow-covered forests. Dividing his forces at the summit, he sent heavier troops down to the River Araxes to cut off the retreat. Then the rest sprinted 9.6km/6 miles uphill to surprise the Persian outposts in the dark. They fled without giving the alarm. At daybreak Alexander attacked the unsuspecting Persians from the rear while Craterus launched a frontal assault. Bewildered, the Persians scattered, jumping from cliffs or being killed trying to flee. The road to Persepolis lay open.

THE WEALTH OF PERSEPOLIS
The palaces of Persia stood on an artificial mound 18m/60ft high in the valley of Mervdasht, then fertile but now arid.

Approached by magnificent staircases were the audience halls of Darius and Xerxes, with the palaces around them. Their brick walls, 20m/65ft high, were covered in gold and glazed tiles, while huge columns with bull-head capitals supported high roofs. Alexander's men had never seen anything like this "richest city under the sun". The Persian governor showed Alexander around the palaces, including the royal treasury, containing 120,000 talents of gold and silver.

Alexander ordered 10,000 pack animals to carry the treasure to Susa for safekeeping and reinstated the Persian governor. Only then did he let his men loot the palaces, producing an orgy of destruction that wrecked many great artworks. Guards and inhabitants were killed indiscriminately until the king ended it. Seeing a statue of Xerxes shattered on the ground, Alexander began to have doubts about how far he could continue a war of revenge. But the greatest destruction was still to come.

BURNING THE PALACES

Among the intrepid women who had accompanied the army from Europe was Thais, the beautiful Athenian mistress of Ptolemy, the general and historian. Ptolemy never mentioned her role in the drunken night that saw the burning of the palaces, but others did. At a banquet

where music played and women such as Thais were present, Alexander and his companions drank heavily. Thais teasingly said it was up to the women to punish the Persians finally for their attack on Greece and burn the palaces. The Companions guffawed approval and Thais, seizing a torch, led a wild procession up the great staircases. First Alexander, then Thais, threw a flaming torch on to the floor of Xerxes' Hundred-Columned Hall. Its cedar-wood columns quickly caught light, as did the other palaces. Soon all were ablaze, as archaeology has confirmed. The Panhellenic crusade had achieved its declared goal.

Above: Darius made Persepolis the ceremonial capital of his immense empire in the 6th century BC, building palaces intended to overawe his subjects with magnificent staircases such as this.

Below: Another view of the palace of Darius I at Persepolis, whose high walls were once covered with glazed and gold tiles.

CHAPTER IV

THE LORD OF ASIA

330–323BC

The capture of Persepolis, followed by the murder of Darius, changed Alexander's policies and attitudes. He no longer saw himself as a Panhellenic leader but as king of Asia, if not exactly Great King. Increasingly, Iranian nobles accepted him as such, but this did not mean an end to his wars.

Persia had left many tribes in remoter eastern provinces unsubjugated – not something Alexander was prepared to do. To be true ruler of all the satrapies, he had to fight guerrilla wars in areas unknown to Greeks. His military genius always won through, but he faced growing problems with his own soldiers. As lord of Asia he had to appear suitably regal, adopting at least some oriental customs. These proved anathema to Macedonian veterans, still the core of his army. In an increasingly tense atmosphere, plots were discovered – or fabricated – that led to old comrades being killed. When Alexander marched yet further east into India, his men finally rebelled.

Robbed of his desire to reach the world's limits (as he understood them), Alexander returned to Babylon, where he died aged not yet 33. Unusually open-minded, he had tried to unite the Persian and Macedonian nobility to create a new ruling class. Although this new elite would speak Greek, the plan led the Macedonians to outright mutiny. Alexander, suppressing this, continued with ever more grandiose plans. These died with him, however, as did all hopes of a united empire.

Left: The pass into Kafiristan among the Hindu Kush mountains, north-western Pakistan.

FROM PERSEPOLIS TO HERAT
330–329BC

Above: Alexander's pothos (longing) for the distant horizon shines through this bust. Wanderlust may explain part of his endless journeying.

Below: A fertile valley in the Elburz Mountains in northern Iran, which the Macedonians crossed in 330BC. The area makes an exception to the aridity of much of the Iranian plateau.

Alexander headed north to Ecbatana (Hamadan) in May 330BC. With a 60,000-strong army, he expected to fight another battle. But although Darius had his eastern satraps' troops and a few Greek mercenaries, he again turned and ran. This time, his irresolution proved fatal. Bessus, a distant relation, seized and deposed him, determined to retreat east to Bactria, his far-off satrapy. In early June, Alexander reached Ecbatana, where he paid off his Greek allies and Thessalian cavalry, officially ending the Panhellenic crusade. Some chose to re-enlist at increased rates; the rest returned home.

DARIUS' DEATH

The moment he heard of Darius' capture, Alexander took 500 horsemen in hot pursuit east beyond Ragae (Tehran). But they caught up with the Persian rebels too late. Bessus, seeing him approach, had murdered Darius, abandoning his baggage to flee east. The body of the last Achaemenid was found in a wagon by a Macedonian, bound in gold chains. When Alexander saw his enemy's corpse, he wrapped it in his own cloak and sent it to Persepolis for royal burial – actions that reveal that he saw himself as Darius' heir.

ALEXANDER HEADS EAST

So, increasingly, did the Persian nobility. As Alexander's army passed through the wooded Elburz Mountains and down to Zadracarta on the Caspian Sea, Persian nobles, including the Grand Vizier implicated in Darius' murder, appeared. Alexander pardoned him and many others. Obviously he needed experienced Persian-speakers (few Macedonians ever spoke much Persian) to run the complex imperial administration.

Artabazus, whom Alexander had met long ago at Pella and whose daughter Barsine had been his mistress, arrived with his seven sons, some of them former satraps. Alexander welcomed them all warmly. Darius' 1,500 Greek hoplites were pardoned and enlisted in the army

– but at the old, lower rate. At Zadracarta Alexander held games by the seaside. His men, relaxing for two weeks, admired this strange sea, which hardly tasted of salt but teemed with fish. Most Greeks thought that the Caspian opened north on to the Ocean, which they regarded as encircling the world. (Unknown to them, the Caspian's north coasts had been discovered under Darius I nearly 200 years before.) The prospect of being so near the world's edge must have aroused Alexander's *pothos* (longing) again. But his route lay south-east into the heartland of old Iran.

A KING TO THE PERSIANS

As the army marched south-east from Meshed into Areia (west Afghanistan), news came that Bessus was "wearing his diadem erect", in other words had proclaimed himself Great King.

Partly in response to this, Alexander now began adopting some aspects of Persian court etiquette to impress his new subjects. These included elements of Persian dress, a sensitive subject to Macedonians, who thought trousers laughably effeminate. Alexander avoided trousers but began wearing a diadem (cloth band) and Persian robes such as a purple-striped tunic. He also introduced Persian court ceremonial, with cup bearers, eunuchs and (reputedly) 365 concubines. Ushers and chamberlains now controlled access to the king, who sat enthroned in splendour. All this differed sharply from the informal Macedonian court, so at first Alexander ran parallel courts, one for Persians, another for Macedonians.

In Ariana, Alexander founded another city, now Herat, and reappointed its satrap Satibarzanes. There were dangers in employing Persians, however, for Satibarzanes at once revolted. Alexander, turning back, defeated his army but Satibarzanes himself escaped with some men.

PHILOTAS AND PARMENION

In September 330BC, Alexander faced trouble closer to home. A plot was uncovered to kill him in which Philotas, son of the veteran general Parmenion and a boyhood friend, was allegedly involved. Found guilty by the Macedonian army, recovering for a moment its old judicial role, Philotas was stoned to death.

Secret orders sent by special couriers then ensured the killing of Parmenion, who was commanding the reserve forces in distant Ecbatana, a position of great power on the route back home. But while Philotas had a trial and execution, if one based on doubtful charges, Parmenion's death has been considered by some historians as tantamount to murder. The elderly general, Philip's old friend, was simply stabbed to death.

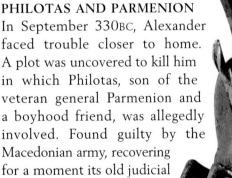

Below: A winged gold ibex of the Achaemenid period. Ibex were common in the remote mountains of Central Asia, the home of independent Iranian barons, whom Alexander had to fight or charm into accepting his rule.

THE ROAD THROUGH OXIANA 329–328 BC

Above: Double bull-headed pillars, typical of Persian architecture's majestic elegance, which Alexander came to appreciate.

The campaigns of the next two years reveal Alexander's unbeatable determination, as he pushed deeper into central Asia. In October 329 BC he entered Drangiana (Halmand), there founding another Alexandria: Kandahar. He decided to approach Bactria, Bessus' huge central Asian satrapy, from the south-east. As always, he chose the hardest route.

As winter deepened, he led 40,000 men up the south flanks of the Hindu Kush, known to Greeks as the Indian Caucasus. Men and horses suffered terribly on the snow-covered slopes of the highest mountains they had yet seen, afflicted by altitude sickness. But, encouraged by their king, who personally helped the stragglers, they marched on. By moving in mid-winter, they surprised hibernating tribesmen who might have harried them – and wrong-footed Bessus. Alexander founded another city, Alexandria-in-the-Caucasus, near Kabul, resting his army before continuing north in early May. A gruelling climb over another spur of mountains brought the army down into Bactria and its chief city of Bactra (Balkh).

DEATH OF BESSUS

Bessus, panicking at Alexander's sudden appearance, fled north to Sogdiana, so losing almost all support. Alexander, cheered by hearing that the treacherous satrap Satibarzanes had been killed, crossed the desert to the Oxus, the huge river dissecting the land. Here he faced a problem: there were no bridges and no timber with which to build any. So he ordered his men to stuff their leather bags with hay and swim across on these. Startled, the Sogdians offered to surrender Bessus, thinking this would end the pursuit. Ptolemy, one of Alexander's chief generals, rode out to collect the captive traitor. Bessus was then displayed naked by the roadside, and repeatedly whipped as the army passed by. Later in Ecbatana he was mutilated and impaled – a punishment Arrian, the philosophically minded historian, damned as barbarous, but which the Persians expected.

DEATH IN SAMARKAND

The Sogdians had expected Alexander to turn back after Bessus' capture, but he marched on towards the River Jaxartes,

Right: Alexander's route east only occasionally followed the obvious roads, as he zigzagged north and south in pursuit of enemies, sometimes retracing his steps. He was always master of the unexpected approach.

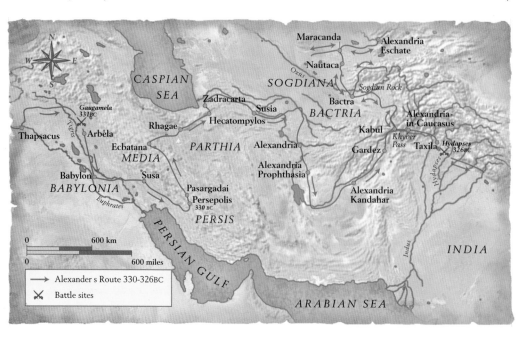

THE CITY-FOUNDER

Alexander is credited with founding at least 18 cities, often replacing older settlements, which may make him the greatest city-founder ever. Some have thrived, others have vanished, and many survive under new names (Kabul, Khojend). Alexandria-in-Egypt, which was new, rapidly became one of the world's greatest cities. The colonists Alexander planted across Asia were mostly soldiers who, because of illness, age or wounds, could not keep up with his unending blitzkriegs. Supplementing this Greek-Macedonian core were varied locals and captives.

After Alexander's death some colonists, who had seldom been volunteers, tried to return home but were forced back to their new cities by Alexander's successors. Whatever Alexander's motives were for these foundations (some people have seen them simply as military bases to control his empire), they helped to spread Hellenism widely, if thinly, across Asia. As the ruins of Ai Khanum in Afghanistan (another Alexandria) show, such cities could boast fine theatres, gymnasia and temples – all considered essential for a Greek *polis*.

Above: Herat in western Afghanistan is one of the 18 cities Alexander founded (or refounded) as military colonies, most of which have since flourished. The cities were planned as typical Greek poleis, each with a theatre, agora, gymnasium, temples and a council.

Below: Often campaigning in mid-winter across high mountains to catch enemies unawares, Alexander and his army had to cross snowed-up passes. Innate Macedonian toughness and Alexander's example kept the army going.

taking Samarkand (Miracanda) en route. The river marked the outer limits of the Persian Empire. Here Alexander founded another city, Alexandria-Eschate (the Furthest), today Khojend. Then rebellion in the rear led by Spitamenes, one of Bessus' associates, forced him to send 2,000 troops to relieve Samarkand.

He himself crossed the Jaxartes to defeat Scythian horsemen on the river's far side, who were hindering his operations. These nomads, cousins of those north of the Black Sea, were duly defeated, but in the desert Alexander contracted dysentery from bad water. In other fights he was wounded twice, once severely. Then came news that Spitamenes had defeated the Samarkand relief force, and Alexander had to gallop madly with some cavalry to save Samarkand. Spitamenes simply vanished into the mountains, involving the Macedonians in protracted guerrilla warfare. When the army returned to Samarkand in late summer 328BC, tempers were frayed, despite the welcome arrival of 21,000 reinforcements (mostly Greek), led by Nearchus, an old friend.

To relax, they drank to excess even by Macedonian standards. (Water in Samarkand was notoriously brackish.) In their drunkenness they quarrelled, resentments at Alexander's orientalizing policies resurfacing. Cleitus the Black, a *hipparch* (cavalry general) who had saved Alexander's life at Granicus, taunted the king, saying that he owed his success to his soldiers and Philip. Enraged, Alexander seized a spear and ran Cleitus through. Then, overcome by remorse at murdering an old friend at dinner, he withdrew to his tent and lay for three days without eating or drinking. Finally his soldiers decided that the anger of Dionysus, the wine god whose festival they had overlooked, lay behind it. This incident reveals Alexander's touchy pride and sometimes homicidal rage.

MARRIAGE ON THE ROCK
327BC

Above: As Alexander marched ever further east, he encountered and conquered ever higher mountains, such as the Kohi-i-Baba range. On one of them he found true love in Roxane.

Below: The wedding of Alexander to Roxane, here painted by the 18th-century Italian artist Marianno Rossi, took place high up on the Sogdian Rock. There were no offspring until a son was born after Alexander's death.

In late 328BC, Alexander's fortunes changed for the better. In November, Spitamenes, whose guerrilla raids had been growing desperate, was killed by his own troops; his severed head was thrown into Alexander's camp. Early in 327BC, Alexander renewed his campaign in eastern Sogdiana, ignoring snow blizzards that claimed the lives of 2,000 men, determined to quash the last opposition.

Near modern Hissar on the Koh-in-Noor mountains, rebels had found refuge in a local baron's castle on the Sogdian Rock, reputedly 3,600m/12,000ft high. When Alexander demanded their surrender, he was told to grow wings and fly. Angered, he chose 300 volunteers to climb by night up the sheer icy rock face. On the climb 30 men died. But, when morning broke, the Sogdians looked up to see what they thought was an army high above them. Overwhelmed, they at once surrendered.

LOVE AT FIRST SIGHT

Among the captives was the stunningly beautiful daughter of Oxyartes (another Sogdian baron), Roxane, whose name meant 'little star'. Alexander fell in love with her at first sight. As she was a captive, he refused to force marriage on her despite the obvious political advantages that would accrue. Luckily, politics and passion coincided, for Roxane accepted him and a sky-high wedding was celebrated on the Rock. The castle held enough supplies to feed an army for two years – a most useful dowry. The newly weds together cut a loaf of bread with Alexander's sword, each then eating one half (an old Persian custom).

Alexander took his army and bride back to Bactra, which he replanned as a splendid Greek city. He also ordered that 30,000 upper-class Persian boys be enrolled for training as soldiers. Their weapons were to be Macedonian and their language Greek. Their families

were given no choice about this conscription, the first of many measures intended to create a united Perso-Macedonian ruling class. The next measure was even more contentious.

THE PAGES' PLOT

The Persians used to offer *proskynesis* (obeisance) to superiors, especially to the Great King, in differing ways according to their own class. This did not entail Persian nobles grovelling on the ground, as later historians supposed, although common people did kowtow, as would special supplicants. Instead, Persian noblemen would bow and, extending their hands, blow a kiss. Their superior would respond by embracing them in ways varying according to rank. All Persians paid *proskynesis* to the Great King, but this implied no worship of the Persian monarch, who was no god. However, *proskynesis* was how the Greeks honoured their gods, not their monarchs, and its prevalence among Persians soon led to serious misunderstandings.

Callisthenes, the campaign's official historian and cousin of Aristotle, used to boast that Alexander would be famous only due to his history. (Ironically, it has since been lost.) In it he had often praised the king as godlike. Among other things he tutored the royal pages, Macedonian boys in their teens, in the same way that

Aristotle had taught Alexander. Most Greek rulers regarded a tame philosopher as essential to court life, and Alexander kept on good terms with Aristotle for a long time. Callisthenes, however, while indisputably learned, was also silly.

Alexander realized that it was galling to Persian nobles to see the Macedonians approach him, their king, with rough informality while they had to make formal obeisance. With some close friends such as Hephaistion he conceived a way to get Macedonians to pay him *proskynesis* too. One night at dinner in Bactra a gold cup filled with wine went around the tables. Each guest, forewarned, stood up, drank a toast and did *proskynesis*, bowing slightly, before going up to receive a kiss on the cheek from Alexander. All went smoothly until the cup reached Callisthenes. He drank, did *not* bow but still expected a kiss, which Alexander refused. "So, I go the poorer by a kiss", Callisthenes said.

Nothing more happened that night. But soon after, when the army was on the move again, a serious conspiracy was discovered among the pages. One boy, Antipater, humiliated by a flogging he had received for killing a boar before Alexander (a major breach of etiquette), formed a plot with friends to kill the king while he slept.

As it happened, Alexander stayed up drinking until dawn so the plot misfired. But, unable to keep quiet, the pages talked about it until it reached the ears of Ptolemy. Arrests, interrogations and torture followed. The pages asserted that Callisthenes had urged them on. He was arrested, tortured and hanged. Whether he was behind the plot remains unknown, but he articulated the anti-Persian attitudes of Greeks and Macedonians, who, feeling they were the victorious master-race, refused to adopt oriental customs.

Plans to introduce *proskynesis* were probably shelved for the time being, as the army turned east towards India, Alexander's next and most adventurous goal.

Left: North of Sogdiana lay steppes inhabited by Scythian and other nomads, whose realm spread across Eurasia to the Black Sea. This gold vase, if Scythian in style and content, may have been made by Greek craftsmen.

Below: Aristotle, Alexander's old tutor, had suggested his relation Callisthenes as the campaign's historian and tutor to the royal pages. But Callisthenes filled the young pages' heads with lofty theories that led them to plot against Alexander and so to their arrest and execution. Callisthenes had already angered the king by refusing to salute him in the Persian manner.

INDIA: THE WORLD'S END
327–326 BC

Above: Alexander attacking Porus, the Indian rajah on an elephant, from a coin struck to celebrate the victory.

Below: If less famous than his battles with the Persians, Hydaspes was perhaps Alexander's finest victory. Facing a superior enemy with elephants across a monsoon-swollen river, Alexander deceived Porus by dividing his forces and taking half of them upstream to cross secretly. His other troops then crossed in direct attack. The resulting battle was hard fought but Porus became a loyal ally.

The Persian Empire had once stretched to the River Indus, but its Indian satrapies (now north-west Pakistan) had long been lost by Alexander's time. India was known to Greeks as a wildly exotic land – filled with gold-hunting ants among other wonders, according to Herodotus – and fabulously rich. Its kingdoms were powerful but divided.

For Alexander, to have refused such a challenge was unthinkable, although he had no idea how huge and varied India really was. There was almost no contact at the time between Greece and India. One problem he did recognize was that of India's elephants, whose smell terrified horses that were unused to them.

The army Alexander led into India in late 327 BC was now half-Asian. He had left many older soldiers in Bactria as settlers or garrisons, recruiting instead 30,000 Bactrian and Sogdian horsemen. While most of the Macedonian infantry had abandoned its long sarissas in favour of shorter, more manageable spears and there had been changes in the army's structure, its core and senior officers remained solidly Macedonian.

STAND-OFF AT THE HYDASPES

The direct route into India lay through the Khyber Pass. But Alexander, wanting to secure his lines of communication, turned left for an arduous campaign against mountain tribes in the wild Chitral and Swat regions.

The climax came early in 326 BC with the capture of the rock-fortress of Aornus on the summit of Pirsar 1,500m/5,000ft above the Indus. Misunderstanding local legends, the Greeks identified a local god as Dionysus, the wine god who had visited India. This misread myth further fuelled Alexander's dreams of conquest.

When the army descended to the Indus, it was welcomed by the ruler of Taxila. This made an enemy in Porus, rajah of Pauravas just to the east. Porus gathered a large army, including 85 elephants, on the east bank of the River Hydaspes (now the Jhelum), which the Macedonians reached in May.

The stand-off resembled that at the River Granicus eight years earlier, but this time Alexander was heavily outnumbered and also faced the challenge of many elephants. The Hydaspes, swollen by recent rains, was also a far more formidable river than the Granicus, being at least 0.8km/½ mile wide.

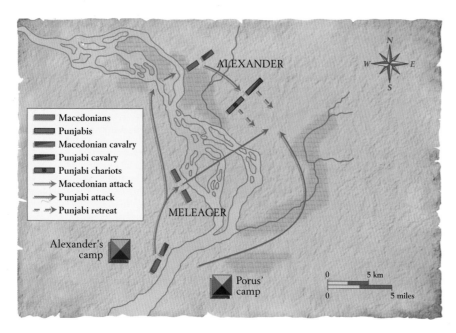

Macedonians
Punjabis
Macedonian cavalry
Punjabi cavalry
Punjabi chariots
Macedonian attack
Punjabi attack
Punjabi retreat

ALEXANDER

MELEAGER

Alexander's camp

Porus' camp

0   5 km
0   5 miles

VICTORY OVER PORUS

Alexander reacted with typical ingenuity. First, he gave the impression that he was making a permanent camp. From it he launched boats on the river every night to exhaust the Indians by constant false alarms. Then, his moves disguised by rain, he secretly divided his forces, leaving Craterus with half the army. He covertly marched his force of 11,000 infantry and 5,000 cavalry 24km/15 miles upriver. Here a wooded island enabled his men to cross by night, the infantry in specially built boats, the horsemen wading through water that rose to their horses' necks. They reformed on the far bank to meet Porus' advance guard coming toward them.

Other Macedonians under Meleager now crossed halfway up the river to catch the Indians on their flank. Alexander deployed his normal oblique attack to devastating effect, his light infantry dispersing to counter the elephants while the cavalry again delivered the knockout blow. After long, hard fighting, Porus' army was routed in perhaps Alexander's most brilliant victory. Alexander, accepting Porus' surrender, restored his old kingdom and generously added to it. In return, Porus became a loyal ally. Alexander struck a series of splendid coins and medals showing elephants and Indian archers. But his appetite for Indian conquests had been sharpened, not sated.

THE ARMY'S REFUSAL

Alexander had heard that east along the Ganges lay the vast but decadent kingdom of Ksandrames, ripe for conquest. East of that must flow the all-encircling Ocean, or so Aristotle had taught. He sacrificed to the Sun and in June began planning the advance from the River Hyphasis (the Beas, east of Amritsar), where his army was encamped. As he did so, the torrential monsoon rains began.

Right: Alexander's army crossing the Indus to fight Porus, an illustration from a medieval French manuscript of Quintus Curtius, one of the ancient histories of Alexander.

The Macedonians had never experienced such deluges. Rivers rose 9m/30ft and burst their banks, and snakes emerged in terrifying numbers. In the wet heat the soldiers' clothes rotted. For men who had marched 19,000km/12,000 miles, it was too much. When Alexander tried to enthuse them about the lands waiting to be conquered, they were silent. Then Coenus, a trusted veteran, voiced the general longing to return home.

Alexander, declaring that he would force no one to follow him but advance alone if needed, retired to his tent – but to no avail. His army was adamant. Finally, reluctantly, furiously, he agreed to return, to his soldiers' tearful joy.

Above: The river Indus rises in the mountains to the north, becoming vast as it enters the plains of Porus' kingdom.

Below: Alexander crowned with victory, a contemporary coin.

THE LONG RETURN
326-325 BC

Returning to the River Hydaspes, Alexander found the fleet that Craterus had prepared, made from timber cut in the Himalayas. Alexander had decided to return not by the same land route but by sailing down the rivers to the Ocean. He left behind two new cities – Nicaea (Victoryville) and Bucephela, commemorating his victory and his beloved horse.

In November 326 BC the army, c.120,000 strong, embarked in a fleet of 800 ships. Alexander "stood in the bows of his ship and poured a libation [offering] into the water from a golden bowl, solemnly invoking the river… After a libation to Hercules his ancestor, Ammon and the other customary gods, he ordered the trumpets to sound and the whole fleet began to move downriver." Hephaistion marched on the left bank and Craterus on the right as flank guards.

A BRUSH WITH DEATH

At first, the voyage seemed an exploratory cruise. Local tribes, overawed by the armada, submitted peacefully, although rapids caused problems for the amateur fleet. (Several galleys, including Alexander's own, were sunk, the king having to swim for his life, but the fleet was reassembled.)

Ahead, the warlike Mallians refused to submit – to Alexander's joy. He surprised them by a cross-desert march, besieging their capital Multan in early 325 BC. The outer city was soon captured but, attacking the citadel, ladders broke, leaving Alexander with three companions on top of the wall. When Alexander jumped down to fight *inside* the walls, an arrow pierced his lung. Peucestas shielded him – with the sacred shield from Troy – until other Macedonians burst in, slaughtering everyone in the city in furious grief that their king had been killed.

In fact, Alexander survived, for his doctor removed the arrowhead. But rumours of his death persisted, so a mere week later he was taken by boat to the camp. To convince his men that he was alive, he not only got up but mounted his horse, "at which the entire army applauded wildly over and over again… pressing against him, touching his hands, knees or clothes". His lung wound proved so bad that he never again walked, let alone fought, without pain. His officers berated him for recklessly endangering his life, and the army's safety, but, as Arrian said, "in truth he was fighting mad… for him the sheer joy of battle was irresistible".

THROUGH THE DESERT

Alexander reached the Indian Ocean in July. Here the fleet was almost wrecked by gigantic storms and surprised by the tides, both unknown in the Mediterranean. He founded another Alexandria as a port, with an eye to India's potential for trade. He sent his new elephant corps and 10,000 veterans back by an easy northerly route, but had

Above: Although severely wounded at the siege of Multan in 325 BC, Alexander still led his men from the front.

Below: The upper reaches of the Indus, the great river down which Alexander and his fleet of 800 ships sailed to the Indian Ocean.

different plans for himself. He intended to march his army through the Gedrosian (Mekran) desert, something never done before even in legend. Meanwhile, Nearchus was to sail the fleet along the coast to the Euphrates, keeping in touch with the army. Like all Greek fleets, Nearchus' ships could not stay long at sea.

At first the army's journey was pleasant: myrrh trees grew so abundantly that the soldiers crushed the precious herb beneath their feet. But soon supplies, especially of water, ran short, and although they often marched by night rather than by day, the heat was overpowering. The men slaughtered and ate their animals, including horses – a lack of discipline that Alexander ignored.

At one stage in the endless desert even their guides got lost and Alexander had to lead the army back down to the coast to find the trail.

Although Alexander now always rode, he shared the hardships in other ways, especially thirst. On one occasion some soldiers, finding a trickle of water, filled a helmet and took it to Alexander, who, wrote Arrian, "with a word of thanks took the helmet and poured the water on the ground in full view of the army. The effect of this action was extraordinary, as if every man in the army had had a good drink… proof not only of his powers of endurance but of his genius in leadership." But this genius did not save thousands from dying. Only about a quarter of the original 40,000-strong army survived – the one true defeat in Alexander's career.

REUNITED WITH NEARCHUS

Reaching the desert's edge after 60 days' march, he sent camels racing ahead to order supplies. Alexander's progress then became a glorious Bacchanalian revel as the army unwound after its ordeal.

Reunited in December 326BC, Alexander wept with joy at seeing his old friend Nearchus again, thanking Zeus and Ammon, saying this reunion gave him more joy than all his conquests. Nearchus, too, had had a hard journey. His sailors had suffered from heat, thirst, hunger and alarming encounters with whales – never seen by Greeks before – and coastal tribes when the sailors had landed looking for water and food. But Nearchus had lost only one ship.

Above: A trireme, the archetypal Greek triple-tiered galley that Alexander's men built even on the shores of the Indus for his fleet that sailed down river to the Indian Ocean.

Below: Alexander decided to return to Persia marching through the centre of the vast Gedrosian (Mekran) desert shown here, an unprecedented venture. He himself survived, but three quarters of his army died in what was his worst, if scarcely known, defeat.

THE WRATH OF THE KING
324 BC

Above: The Heraion, the main temple on Samos. Alexander's decree that all Greek exiles should return caused huge problems for Athens, which had settled many colonists on the island.

Below: On his return to Persia Alexander found that the tomb at Pasargadae of Cyrus the Great, founder of the Persian Empire, had been desecrated. He had the tomb's priestly guardians executed, commissioning the architect Aristobolus to restore it.

Few of the governors appointed by Alexander, Persian or Macedonian, had ever expected to see him alive again. Fourteen of the empire's 23 satrapies were showing signs of revolt. Rumours of Alexander's near-fatal wounding at Multan, then his disappearance into the desert, had encouraged even an old friend such as Harpalus, imperial treasurer, to act independently – he had begun minting his own coins in Babylon. Alexander, as the news reached him, reacted by launching a reign of terror. In it many governors, soldiers and officials were executed for corruption or disloyalty, including 600 Thracian mercenaries who had abused their power in Media. Harpalus fled to Athens, taking his two mistresses and 6,000 talents with him, money later used to finance the anti-Macedonian cause.

PASAGARDAE AND PERSEPOLIS
Dismissing Nearchus, who sailed on to the Euphrates, Alexander continued into Persia proper. Revisiting Pasargadae, the capital of Cyrus the Great, which he had

seen briefly in 330 BC, he was horrified to discover that Cyrus' tomb had been desecrated, allegedly by its priestly guardians. Alexander had these Magi tortured but learnt nothing. He ordered Aristobulus, an architect-biographer, to restore the tomb completely. The task took Aristobulus many years, but the restored tomb still stands. Moving on to Persepolis early in 324 BC, Alexander gazed at the blackened ruins of the palaces, perhaps now regretting that drunken night's destruction six years before.

ADOPTING PERSIAN CUSTOMS
Now he was concerned to gain the loyalty of the Persian nobility, crucial to running the empire. Personal feelings were not wholly absent, however. Bagoas, his Persian lover, for some reason hated Orsines, the aristocratic Persian governor of Persis. So Alexander had Orsines stripped of his rank and crucified without trial, his place being taken by Peucestas.

Peucestas, who had saved Alexander's life at Multan, was unusual among Macedonians in having learned Persian. He followed his king in adopting modified Persian court dress. This was what Alexander wanted all his officers to do, although most grumbled about copying slavish barbarian habits. The king had his eyes on the future, however. Reunited with Nearchus and other companions in April 324 BC at Susa – whose Persian governor he imprisoned for corruption – he announced perhaps his most ambitious plan, concerning love more than war.

THE MARRIAGES OF SUSA
Alexander took two new wives – the daughters respectively of Darius and of Artaxerxes III, an earlier Great King. Persia's kings traditionally were even more polygamous than Macedonia's. Hephaistion married another princess,

THE PYRE OF CALANUS

Alexander was no "stranger to the loftier flights of philosophy, though the slave of his own ambition" in Arrian's words. Intrigued in 326BC at Taxila by *gymnosophists* (ascetics who had renounced wordly ambition), he asked some to accompany

his army. Only one did, Calanus, becoming Alexander's close friend. When the army reached Persepolis in 324BC, Calanus, "who had never been sick in all his life", fell seriously ill. He decided to end his life despite Alexander's entreaties. Ptolemy was told to prepare a pyre and Calanus was "escorted to it by a solemn procession of horses, men, soldiers … bearing cups of gold and silver and royal robes." As the flames mounted, Alexander, who "felt there was something indecent in witnessing such a friend's ordeal" ordered trumpets to sound and men to raise the battle-cry. Even the elephants joined in a noisy farewell to the man whose ideals were so very different from a world-conqueror's.

Left: Calanus, the Indian gymnosophist (fakir), who had followed Alexander, decided to die on a pyre when the army reached Persepolis in 324BC.

Above: Alexander dressed as Ares, the god of war, in a fresco from Pompeii – copying a Hellenistic original – showing his marriage to Statira, daughter of Darius III, in 324BC.

while 80 of the most senior officers also took high-ranking Persian wives. Alexander then gave official blessing to about 10,000 of his men's unions with Asian women, with sizeable gifts. Children of these mixed marriages would be Macedonian, the nucleus of a Perso-Macedonian ruling class.

RESTRUCTURING THE ARMY

He took his army north to Opis on the Euphrates in June. There he greeted as 'successors' the 30,000 Persian youths trained as Macedonian soldiers so that they could integrate seamlessly with the rest of the infantry. Noble Iranians such as Roxane's brother were enrolled in the crack Companion Cavalry, while 10,000 older Macedonians were to be honourably discharged and sent home.

These moves caused widespread mutiny. "Go and conquer with your daddy Ammon," some soldiers jeered, deeply affronting Alexander. Ordering the arrest and execution of 13 of the

ringleaders, he declared they would still be "poor beggars in animal skins" without his father's and especially his leadership. Then he dismissed the whole army, appointing Persians to every post.

Stunned, the soldiers begged his forgiveness. There followed a tearful reconciliation, a banquet at which Alexander prayed for *omonia* (harmony) between Persians and Macedonians – and the veterans went off after all. Exactly as Alexander wanted.

Right: Back in Persia, Alexander adopted many luxurious Persian customs to impress his Asian subjects. The Persian crown had become hugely wealthy, as this gold rhyton indicates.

THE FINAL YEAR
323BC

Above: Alexander wearing a lion-head helmet, one of the many heroic images made after his death.

In August 324BC Alexander issued an edict ordering Greek cities to take back all their exiles. This decree, announced at the Olympic Games, was applauded but caused turmoil in Greece. Many exiles had been wandering the world for years, often as mercenaries. There was often no room for them at home, especially in Athens. The city faced the prospect of thousands of *cleruchs* who had settled in Samos returning if Samian exiles regained their lands. Athens sent several embassies to the king to remonstrate. But Alexander was now little concerned with the plight of distant Greek cities, as he moved among the great capitals of his empire.

More Persians than Macedonians now held prominent posts at court and in the army, both of which looked ever more oriental. Alexander sat on a golden throne wielding a golden sceptre; his royal tent was supported by golden pillars; 500 Persian Immortals matched the 500 Macedonian Companions; and bilingual ushers, staff bearers and concubines thronged the court. Balancing such oriental splendours, many Greeks –

Above: The great stone lion outside Ecbatana (Hamadan) where Hephaistion, Alexander's oldest friend, died in 324BC. It was possibly erected to honour Hephaistion.

actors, poets, secretaries, philosophers, engineers, doctors – found employment at the new king of Asia's court.

THE LOSS OF HEPHAISTION

By October the court was in Ecbatana, the old Median capital. Here Hephaistion, Alexander's vizier, or second in command, fell ill and died, probably of typhoid. No matter that their passions had cooled since boyhood love and that Bagoas was a younger, presumably more attractive rival: Alexander plunged into an orgy of grief.

He crucified Hephaistion's unfortunate physician – Hephaistion, apparently recovering, had ignored the doctor's veto on drinking wine – and threw himself on to the corpse. He shaved his head and had the manes and tails of his horses clipped. (Achilles, his hero, had similarly mourned his lover Patroclus.) He sent messengers to Siwah, sanctuary of Zeus-Ammon his father, to ask how he should honour his dead friend. The answer came back: "as a semi-divine hero". A pyre costing an

Below: A bull from the Gate of Ishtar in Babylon, the city to which Alexander returned in 323BC and where he died.

unprecedented 10,000 talents was prepared in Babylon and funeral games involving 3,000 contestants were staged. A great stone lion which is still standing was probably erected outside Ecbatana in Hephaistion's memory. Then Alexander sought consolation in his favourite activity: war. A winter campaign against the Cosseans, a primitive mountain tribe, provided his last triumph.

PLANNING THE NEXT CAMPAIGN

The Persian kings had avoided Babylon's boiling summers whenever possible. But as the weather warmed up in early 323BC, the court moved down to what was still the greatest city in the empire. Alexander had decided to make Babylon his main capital, partly because it was on a navigable river leading to the sea, so well sited for trade. Unlike the Persians, he never despised commerce. He had the Euphrates and Tigris rivers cleared of dams and ordered the construction of huge docks in Babylon.

Alexander began planning his next campaign of combined discovery and conquest around the Arabian peninsula, rich in spices yet still almost unknown. He intended to lead this himself, but also planned an expedition north to explore the Caspian Sea. Envoys from across the world saluted him outside Babylon. Some were from Carthage – a city he probably intended to conquer – but there were also Scythians, Etruscans, Celts, Ethiopians, Libyans and Iberians. (Rome, however, was probably still too small to be involved.) But he ignored Chaldean priests, who warned him against entering Babylon, saying the omens were bad. He knew these priests had embezzled money that he had earmarked for rebuilding their great temples.

Alexander also proclaimed his own deification, perhaps encouraged by delegates from the Ionian Greek cities. This was unusual but not unprecedented. Lysander the Spartan general had earlier been hailed as a god, as had Dion the Sicilian politician, and Alexander had far

exceeded their achievements. At dinner parties he now began wearing divine robes, which shocked some people but again was not totally unprecedented.

DEATH IN BABYLON

But real gods are immortal. Alexander reputedly attended several hard-drinking parties in May that took him 36 hours to sleep off. At the end of the month Medius, a Thessalian noble, gave a particularly riotous party. Afterwards, Alexander took to his bed with a fever that steadily worsened. The troops, alarmed at his absence, insisted on being admitted to his bedroom. He acknowledged each with a movement of the eyes. Three days later, on 10 June 323BC, Alexander died, aged not yet 33, after a reign of 12 years and 9 months.

Rumours soon circulated that he had been poisoned, possibly with strychnine, by Macedonians alarmed at his orientalizing of the monarchy. Far more probably he died of a marsh fever hitting a constitution already much weakened by wars, numerous wounds and excessive drinking. He left behind a stunned world and no obvious heir to his huge empire. When asked who should succeed him, he had mouthed only the reply: "the strongest".

Above: Alexander's grand entry into Babylon, the destined capital of his empire, as envisaged by the French painter Charles Lebrun.

Below: Mourning for Alexander was widespread. He was long remembered as a semi-legendary figure across half Asia, as this Bukhara miniature from 1533 shows.

ALEXANDER'S LEGACY
A MILITARY GENIUS

Few individuals have had as great an impact on world history as Alexander; fewer still have generated so much controversy, arousing reactions ranging from adulatory enthusiasm to stark disgust. For some 20th-century historians he was a Greek precursor of tyrants such as Hitler, Mao or Stalin. Ernst Badian, voicing such views, described Alexander at his life's end thus: "After fighting, scheming and murdering in pursuit of... power, Alexander found himself at last on a lonely pinnacle over an abyss with no use for his power and security unattainable." For other, more romantic, historians, Alexander was a chivalrous superman, spreading Hellenic civilization but free of Greek racism. With such divergent views, it can be hard to discern the man from the myth.

Above: Of all the cities founded by Alexander, none surpassed Alexandria-in-Egypt, soon one of the richest and most sophisticated cities on earth. Its greatest building was the huge pharos *(lighthouse), whose light could be seen 50km/31 miles away.*

Above: Alexander as Helios Cosmocrator, omnipotent sun god, in this 1st century BC medallion. He became the archetypal god-king, aped but never equalled by Hellenistic and Roman successors.

THE SPREAD OF HELLENISM

One achievement is indisputable: Alexander vastly extended the Greek world. "We Greeks sit around the sea like frogs around a pond," Plato had said, noting how Greek cities, while spread around the Mediterranean, clung to the coasts. But after Alexander's conquests, Hellenism exploded eastwards, producing a cultural diffusion with profound consequences. Centuries later art in India, central Asia and even China would show the impact of Greek ideals of the human form. While Alexander did not plan this, it was the result of his conquests.

Below: Alexander was portrayed in many different guises, even rather improbably here as the rustic god Pan.

If politically Alexander wanted a Perso-Macedonian fusion – an enlightened policy abandoned by his successors – he remained Hellenic in culture. He might wear half-Persian clothes and employ Persian nobles, but he hardly (if at all) spoke Persian. In religion also he remained Greek, as in his attitude to cities and trade. The Persians had founded only a few cities as military bases, distrusting merchants. But most of Alexander's cities were founded as true *poleis*. Trade often concerned Alexander, for he founded Alexandria-in-Egypt and another city at the mouth of the Euphrates. As Greek colonists transformed the cities of western Asia, Greek became the common tongue from the Aegean to central Asia.

The immediate results of Alexander's conquest were power and riches on an intoxicating scale for his successors. He had spent 10,000 talents (ten times the annual revenue of classical Athens at its height) just on Hephaistion's funeral – a sign of the rich new world he had opened up. The scale of his achievement long remained unrivalled.

ALEXANDER'S EXTREMISM

Personally Alexander was a man of extremes in almost everything – fighting, feasting, drinking, weeping – except sex. Probably bisexual like many Greeks, he had at least two mistresses, three wives and two male lovers, but was always keener on war than love. He was a fighter before all else.

His ambition, his *pothos* (longing) for conquest, led to the deaths of hundreds of thousands of people. If he had lived, he was not intending to rule his empire in peace. "He would not have stopped conquering even if he had added Europe to Asia and the British Isles to Europe," wrote Arrian. "On the contrary, he would have sought unknown lands beyond them, for it was always his nature… to strive for the best."

Such Homeric striving was heroic but hardly statesmanlike. His chosen role models – Achilles the pugnacious prince, the muscle-bound demigod Hercules, Dionysus the god of wine – suggest he was starting to believe in his own myths.

In the real world, Alexander can be blamed for not leaving an heir – preferably fathered in Macedonia before he even set out for Asia. He must partly be blamed for the chaos that shattered his empire after his death, which might have come far sooner. From the Battle of Granicus to the siege of Multan, Alexander recklessly endangered his life. He was lucky to have lived so long.

Above: Alexander's most notable achievement was his overthrow of the Persian Empire, epitomized in these fallen bull-head capitals. But his visionary plan to unite the Persian and Macedonian nobility in a new ruling class died with him.

THE LEGEND OF ALEXANDER

The myth of the undefeated super-hero soon eclipsed any personal failings. His successors, mostly Macedonian generals, obviously looked back to him, repeating his gestures if not his brilliance. Ptolemy I of Egypt, for example, minted magnificent coins showing Alexander as Ammon. The Romans also became obsessed by Alexander's legend.

Julius Caesar wept when he saw a statue of Alexander and realized that, at the age the young conqueror was already dead, he had achieved nothing memorable. Pompey, Caesar's rival, also imitated Alexander both in his rather absurd bouffant hairstyle and in calling himself Magnus (the Great).

The less flamboyant first emperor Augustus, after defeating Cleopatra VII, last of Alexander's successors, laid a wreath on Alexander's tomb in Alexandria in 30BC in homage. In AD216 the manic emperor Caracalla, opening the same tomb, seized Alexander's armour, which he wore for his own projected attack on the east. (Caracalla was murdered soon after.) Centuries later the first Holy Roman Emperor Charlemagne (reigned 768–814) consciously copied Alexander. A thousand years after that, Napoleon I always travelled with a portrait of Alexander. He is still widely admired for his undoubted military genius, the greatest in antiquity.

Above: Posthumous coin struck for Alexander the Great after his death in 323BC.

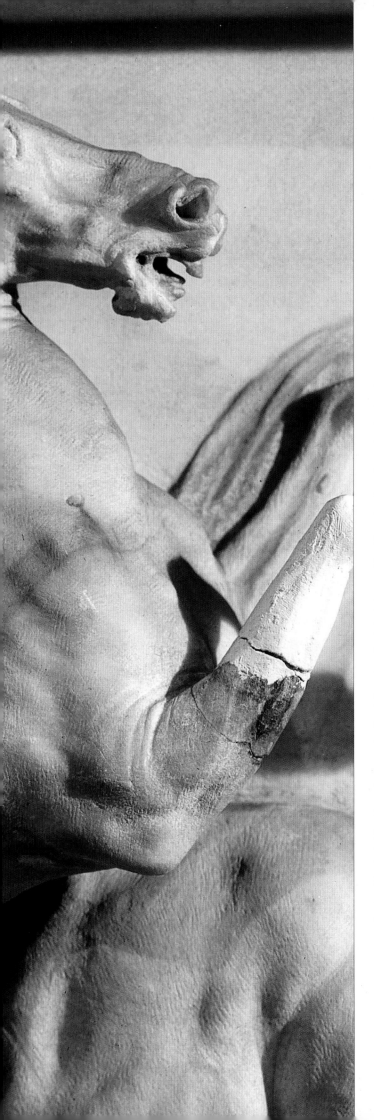

CHAPTER V

ARMS AND ARMOUR

c.2000BC–AD138

Although the classical Greeks were often at war, and almost every citizen served at times as a soldier, they long remained mostly amateur fighters. War between each Greek *polis* (citizen-state) involved citizens directly, at least until mercenaries became common. So when citizens voted for a war, they were putting their own and their families' lives at risk. Even Sparta, that militaristic state, seldom started wars enthusiastically.

Greek warfare centred on set battles between hoplites, heavy infantrymen fighting in line. Hoplites were enrolled from citizen-farmers able to afford their own armour. Cavalry, recruited from the rich, was relatively unimportant. The many poorer citizens provided irregular troops and, in Athens, the crucial rowers for triremes, the triple-tiered galleys. (Slaves were seldom used for these, as they required feeding all year.) Hoplites and triremes proved a winning combination. They repelled the Persian invasions and the Carthaginians in the west. But they were later outclassed by the large professional armies of Macedonia and later monarchies, who deployed cavalry on a regal scale, elephants as tanks and more powerful catapults. They also built far bigger galleys. But ultimately even they could not counter the rising power of Rome.

Left: Alexander, shown on the Sidon Sarcophagus, *loved battles. He was primarily a cavalry commander.*

THE HOPLITE
THE ARCHETYPAL GREEK SOLDIER

Above: An Athenian ephebe *(young man) pouring a libation. Military training in Athens was standardized only in the mid-4th century* BC. *Earlier the Athenian army, if at times successful, was amateur compared to its fleet or to Sparta's army.*

Below: The superb discipline of Spartan hoplites repels a charge by Thessalian horsemen. Constantly drilled, Spartans for centuries made the best hoplites in Greece, distinguished by their scarlet tunics and the Lambda (L) on their shields (for Lacedaemonia, the name of the Spartan state).

Although Homer's legendary heroes had ridden out to individual combat in chariots, chariot warfare probably never developed in Bronze Age Greece because of its mountainous terrain and small plains. Even Homer's heroes in *The Iliad* had to dismount to fight on foot. But light-armed guerilla-style troops were seldom very important either.

For the central centuries of Greek history, wars were decided by heavy infantry in set battles. These gave the victor control of the fertile farmland around each *polis*, which was absolutely vital to a city's existence.

The key Greek foot soldier throughout Greek history was the hoplite (from *hoplos*, shield or armour). These heavily armoured spear men, fighting in close formation, dominated Greek warfare from *c*.700BC until Rome's final conquest of Greece in the 2nd century BC. Hoplites, emerging as the archetypal Greek soldier by *c*.700BC, were recruited from middle-class farmers who owned 2–4ha/5–10 acres of land. Typically, these made up about 35 per cent of the *polis'* population.

ARMOUR

What hoplites wore in battle became almost a uniform. However, as each man supplied his own armour, there were considerable variations, depending on the citizen's wealth. Equipment, a major expense, was handed down from father to son if in good repair. The earliest, and among the most complete, surviving suit of hoplite armour is that of the Panoply Grave at Argos in the Peloponnese from *c*.720BC. The solid bronze cuirass (body armour) has a front and back plate, with the front plate fitting over the back plate's edges. The breastplate attempts to follow the contours of the body beneath, but a lining of some sort was presumably worn. Later, reinforced linen cuirasses became common, which were cheaper and lighter than metal cuirasses. Great men such as King Philip II had iron cuirasses decorated with gold.

Greaves (leg-guards made of bronze or iron and padded with leather) protected legs up to the knees. Helmets gradually evolved into the standard 'Corinthian type', which covered all the face, leaving mere slits for the eyes and mouth. It gave excellent protection for the head but made it hard for the wearer to hear orders. A new type of helmet, the 'Chalcidian', was therefore developed, which left openings around the ears. All helmets had crests of horsehair to make hoplites look taller and more imposing.

The hoplite carried a large shield, about 1m/3ft across and weighing at least 9kg/20lb. Made of wood but edged and faced in bronze, this was held with a single handgrip. Carried on the left arm, it defended the fighter's left side well but his right not at all. This made every hoplite dependent on his right-hand companion not breaking rank in the battle line. Training was needed to keep *en taxei* (in line – modern Greek for 'okay').

The result was a much more disciplined if less glamorous form of fighting than that of *The Iliad*.

WEAPONS

The hoplite's key weapon was his thrusting spear, called a sarissa, originally about 2.7m/9ft long. He also carried a sword about 60cm/2ft long as a cutting weapon for close fighting. Hoplites, massed eight and sometimes 16 men deep, relied on the initial shock of their charge to break the enemy line. If this failed, they turned to shoving and jostling, poking their spears either down at the neck of their opponents or up under their cuirasses.

LORDS OF THE BATTLEFIELD

πExperienced hoplites were seen as lords of the battlefield, and not just in Greece. The defeat of larger Persian armies – at Marathon (490BC) and Plataea (479BC) – by Greek hoplites revealed their supremacy over Persian infantry and cavalry. Greek hoplites were employed as mercenaries by the Egyptian pharaohs in the 6th century BC and by the Persian kings after 401BC, when the rebel Prince Cyrus 'marched upcountry' with the 10,000 mercenaries, as related by Xenophon in

his *Anabasis*. The phalanx, the standard formation for hoplites, changed only slowly over the years. In later versions, which were pioneered by Epaminondas of Thebes in the 370s BC and developed by Philip II of Macedonia (359–336BC), hoplites were massed up to 50 men deep, hugely increasing their impact in full frontal charge. The length of their spears also increased – finally up to 6m/20ft – while shields shrank to about 60cm/3ft and were slung from the neck. In the Macedonian phalanx, both hands were needed to hold a sarissa, but only the first five or six ranks' spears projected. The rest remained upright, helping to shield against arrows. When sarissas were swayed en masse, they made a threatening swooshing sound. But a deep phalanx was unwieldy on uneven battlefields This led to defeats by Rome's more versatile legions at Cynoscephalae in 197BC, Magnesia in 190BC and Pydna in 168BC – battles that marked the end of hoplite warfare.

Left: A Greek hoplite and a cowering Persian archer who has lost his bow. The Greeks' recent defeat of the Persians at Plataea had boosted their military pride, but the Persians were never negligible foes.

Below: Hoplites fighting in formation, from a Corinthian vase of c.600BC. The 'hoplite revolution' had recently made these heavy infantrymen central to Greek warfare, but most armies remained glorified militias. Sparta was the outstanding exception.

CAVALRY AND IRREGULARS
HORSEMEN, SLINGERS AND ARCHERS

Aristotle thought that cavalry had once formed the Greeks' main fighting force, but he was probably mistaken. The *hippeis* (knights) retained their upper-class status in Athens, but lack of decent pasture always prevented cavalry from dominating warfare in Greece proper. Horses remained a luxurious status symbol. The Spartans, egalitarian in their militaristic way, used horses only to carry hoplites into battle. Cavalry was at times employed for scouting and to harry or pursue defeated infantry, but its total numbers remained small.

Plataea, the great land victory in 479BC over the Persians, was won despite the Greeks' lack of cavalry versus mounted Persian troops. This reinforced Greek views that cavalry hardly mattered. Even at Chaeronea in 338BC, when Philip II crushed the armies of Athens and Thebes, the main fighting was done by hoplites, despite Alexander's dashing cavalry charge. In the open spaces of Sicily, however, cavalry could prove useful: at the siege of Syracuse (415–413BC) the Athenians suffered from lack of horsemen to counter harrying Sicilian cavalry.

In Thessaly and Macedonia, lands of relatively spacious plains, cavalry always counted for far more. Significantly, these were lands where aristocracy and monarchy long survived. Alexander employed cavalry as his main aggressive arm (his 'hammer') in his Asiatic campaigns, but the infantry phalanx remained the 'anvil' needed to finish off the Persians.

LACK OF STIRRUPS

There was a technical reason why cavalry was less important in the ancient world: stirrups had not been invented. This made charging with a lance tricky, for the shock of impact threatened to unseat the rider. However, Thessalian and Macedonian horsemen used long spears, also called sarissas, with cornel-wood hearts. Such cavalry were used as his shock troops by Alexander, charging the enemy ranks directly – but Alexander's main victories were against Asian cavalry, not Greek hoplites. Highly experienced riders simply learned to grip harder with their legs to stay on. Philip II increased the number of elite Companion cavalry from only 600 at the start of his reign in 359BC to *c.*4,000 by the end, financed by his remarkable conquests.

THE COMPANION CAVALRY

Alexander's Companion cavalry was divided into eight squadrons (*ilai*) of 200 men commanded by an *ilarch*. The royal *ila* commanded by Alexander was larger at *c.*300 men. Their novel wedge-shaped formations had two advantages: they could break

Below: Alexander personally commanded his cavalry, his royal ila *(squadron) of c.300 horsemen, often spearheading the attack in battle. This triumphant statue is by the 17th-century French sculptor Pierre Puget, hence the anachronistic stirrups.*

through the enemy ranks and they could deploy laterally, greatly increasing their effective power.

Besides Macedonian and Thessalian horsemen, 900 light Thracian and Paeonian mounted scouts accompanied Alexander into Asia in 334BC.

CAVALRY ARMOUR

According to Xenophon, writing c.380BC, a cavalryman wore a cuirass with protection for the thighs, a guard for the left, unshielded, arm and a 'Boeotian' helmet giving good all-round vision. (He advocated riders slinging javelins rather than using lances.) Horses themselves were normally unarmoured. Possibly some Persian cavalry ranked as cataphracts (heavy armoured horsemen), such as the units from Bactria under Bessus at the battle of Gaugamela in 331BC, but most horsemen at this time were light cavalry.

PELTASTS, SLINGERS AND ARCHERS

At the other social extreme to the cavalry, and far more numerous, were the citizens who could not afford hoplite armour. Most served as light-armed troops called peltasts, after the pelta, the light wicker-work shield they carried. This was cut out on top to improve visibility. Their minimal armour was based on Thracian originals. In battle they fought as skirmishers, harrying the enemy with javelins before the main hoplite forces met, then falling back, sometimes sheltering behind the hoplites' shields.

Greece's mountainous terrain might have encouraged more frequent use of such mobile irregulars, but in practice they remained marginal. In 426BC the Athenian general Demosthenes saw his hoplites worsted by peltasts in remote Aetolia. He adopted their tactics to devastating effect on the island of Sphacteria in 425BC, where 292 Spartiate hoplites had to surrender to light troops. In 390BC another Athenian general, Iphicrates, defeated a regiment of 600 Spartan hoplites near Corinth by having

his peltasts provoke them to break ranks and charge out. But although this won Iphicrates great acclaim, it did not seriously affect Sparta's power.

There were also slingers and archers, considered almost cowardly fighters because they did not close up with the enemy like proper hoplites. By the late 5th century BC Cretan and Scythian archers were being employed as mercenaries, using composite bows of bone, horn, wood and sinew. These had a maximum range of c.140m/150 yards. Slingers were also increasingly used, those from Rhodes being considered the best. Later the Balearic Islands provided many slingers. At up to 280m/300 yards, a sling's range was greater than a bow's and it could fire stone, clay or lead shot, of which the last was particularly lethal. Philip and Alexander used numerous Thracian slingers in their armies.

Above: A mounted archer riding bareback, from an Attic red-figure plate, c.520–510BC.

Below: Lighter-armed troops such as peltasts played an increasingly important part if secondary role in battles from the 4th century BC onwards.

AMATEURS AND PROFESSIONALS
TRAINING AND FORMATIONS

Above: The 'Corinthian'- style hoplite helmet of the classical period gave excellent protection if limited vision.

Below: Hoplites fighting at close quarters. Each large round shield gave good protection to the man to the left but each man's right flank was left exposed. Hence the importance of drilling to keep en taxei, in line, something at which Spartans excelled.

Only two Greek armies before the rise of Macedonia could be called professional: the Spartans and later, for a few decades in the 4th century BC, the Thebans. All the rest were citizen-militias of varying degrees of proficiency. Two years' part-time military training on the basis of the tribe was the norm in Athens, and probably elsewhere. But adult citizen-hoplites must have practised the all-important keeping *en taxei*, 'in line', perhaps in their local gymnasium. (In Switzerland, the one modern democracy remotely comparable to ancient Greece, citizen-soldiers still train every year for a few weeks.)

EPHEBES

By the 4th century BC training for young Athenian citizens had become standardized. *Ephebes* (male citizens aged 18–20) were enrolled under ten *sophronistai* (drill masters), one for each tribe. A *kosmetes*

> ### SPARTAN DISCIPLINE
> On land, Spartans were the only professionals before Philip II. Xenophon, the Athenian who settled in Lacedaemonia, gave an enthusiastic account of Spartan *askesis* (discipline). This started in infancy and continued full-time throughout a Spartan's life – something no other city could afford without enslaved *helots* to work their farms. Xenophon praised the way in which Spartan hoplites, if their ranks were broken, could swiftly reform the line, even with Spartans they did not know, and form up from a column on the march to meet sudden frontal or flank attack. Thucydides, less uncritically, admired the efficient Spartan system for passing orders down the line from commander to platoon level.

(marshal) elected by the Assembly super- vised them. *Ephebes* did a year's duty in guard-houses in Piraeus and along the borders, where they learned to fire bows and javelins and use rudimentary artillery, and to fight in line. *Ephebes* of each tribe ate together in barrack messes. At the year's end they appeared before the Assembly, where they proudly displayed their new skills.

Athens could field about 30,000 hoplites in the mid-5th century BC, but these were not fully professional, as defeats from Delium in 424BC by the Thebans to Crannon in 322BC, another Macedonian victory, revealed.

NAVAL STRENGTH

Athens' navy was the city's professional force, the one such navy in classical times. Although founded only in 483BC at Themistocles' urging – its half-trained crews repulsed the Persian fleet at Salamis in 480BC however – it soon became highly professional. By the time of the victory at Eurymedon in 467BC, Athens had gained naval supremacy across the eastern Mediterranean. Each trireme's 170 rowers, recruited from the poorer citizens of Athens and other cities, became skilled, serving under professional *trierarchs* (captains) and helmsmen.

The efficiency of Athens' trireme fleets was stunningly displayed when the *strategos* Phormion defeated a larger Peloponnesian force in 429BC in the Corinthian Gulf. The Athenians drove the enemy ships into a defensive circle with bows pointed outwards. They then rowed closer and closer around until their back-paddling enemies' oars became fatally entangled with each other. Athens' thalassocracy (sea power) was unchallenged until its catastrophic defeat in Sicily in 413BC, when it lost nearly 300 ships with their skilled crews. But triremes, cramped and unseaworthy, could not stay long at sea, and needed to be beached almost every night.

SPARTAN ARMY STRUCTURE

According to Xenophon, every unit in the Spartan army, no matter how small, had its own officer. The basic unit was the *enomotia* of 36 men, four being grouped into a *lochos* (band) of 144 men, commanded by a *lochagos*. Four *lochoi* made up a division, commanded by a *polemarch* (warlord), with six such divisions in the Spartan army proper. There were few full Spartiates by the 4th century BC, however, the core army being supplemented by Peloponnesian allies. On the march, each Spartiate was accompanied by a *helot* carrying his supplies of barley, cheese, onions and salted meat. Greeks, unlike Romans, did not regularly make their camps into one-night forts.

Right: Spartan discipline had its finest hour at Thermopylae in 480BC, when Leonidas and the 300 fought to the last against the Persian hosts, a scene that inspired the French artist Jacques-Louis David 2,400 years later.

THEBES' SACRED BAND

Although little is known of early Thebes, it is clear that it too had well-trained hoplites. At Plataea in 479BC, the Thebans (fighting on Persia's side) resisted the allied Greek army stubbornly, its elite Sacred Band dying to a man.

After Thebes' liberation from Spartan occupation in 378BC, its great general Epaminondas thoroughly reorganized the Theban army, making it into a first-class fighting machine, capitalizing on an upsurge of Theban patriotism. In particular, he increased the depth of the phalanx to 50 on the traditionally weaker left wing – a stroke of genius that defeated the Spartans at Leuctra in 371BC and in several later contests.

He also resuscitated or reorganized the Sacred Band, so that it now consisted of 150 male lovers bound to each other in love and death, making them the best soldiers in Greece. Whether he changed Thebans' actual arms and armaments, perhaps anticipating the smaller Macedonian hoplite shield slung from the neck, remains unknown.

Above: Not all military service was fighting or drilling. These two hoplites are playing keritizein, *a hockey-like game, with their spears.*

GREEK WARSHIPS
PENTECONTERS AND TRIREMES

Above: Quinqueremes were the largest galleys that were practical, used from the 4th century BC onwards by Macedonian and later by Roman generals until the Battle of Actium in 31BC.

All Greek warships, like those of every other Mediterranean state until AD1600, were galleys. Galleys carried sails for voyages, but the nature of naval warfare meant that warships always needed huge numbers of rowers in battle. Lacking effective artillery, fights consisted of closing with the enemy and ramming or boarding. For this, concentrated bursts of powered speed, which massed rowers alone could provide, were essential. In a trireme (the archetypal Greek galley), 170 of the 200 crew were rowers, about 15 were marines (soldiers) and the remainder sailors.

PENTECONTERS AND BIREMES
Early galleys, copying Phoenician models, were penteconters rowed by 50 men. These were the ships, described by Homer, in which Odysseus sailed – and ended up shipwrecked. Built of pinewood with spruce oars, penteconters had removable masts that slotted into the keel. They were steered by oars at the stern, rudders being unknown, with bronze-clad rams. As rowers' open benches offered no comfort and galleys carried little water, ships were beached at night and during the winter. The Phoenicians added a second row of oars over the first, creating faster biremes.

TRIREMES AND LARGER GALLEYS
In the mid-6th century BC biremes were superseded by triremes with three tiers of oars, the topmost supported on an outrigger. A standard Athenian trireme was *c.*37m/121ft long and *c.*5.5m/18ft wide at outrigger level. Oars were *c.*4.5m/15ft long and almost certainly all the same length. There were 27 rowers on each side on the lowest tier, working their oars through portholes close to the water, and 27 rowers on the middle tier. The top ranks of 31 men rowed through an outrigger. Rowers were close-packed inside the hull, the lower ones having their noses almost in the bottoms of those above and in front. (The smell was noted by Aristophanes, the comedian.) Each galley had two anchors at the bow and two steering oars at the stern.

Triremes dominated Greek naval warfare until the development of quinqueremes in the mid-4th century BC. These either had two extra tiers or two men pulling each oar.

Even larger galleys are recorded, with 10, 12 and even 40 tiers of rowers. But such vessels were increasingly unwieldy. After Rome's victory over Cleopatra and Antony's mostly quinquereme fleet at Actium in 31BC, biremes again became the norm in the Mediterrenean.

Below: Another view of triremes. In battle, a galley's sails were stowed away, as triremes fought mainly by ramming enemy ships.

BATTLE TACTICS

A vital crew member was the flautist, who piped time for the rowers. Keeping time required much practice, but a well-trained trireme crew created a formidable fighting machine. This could reach maximum speeds of 24kph/15mph over short distances, accelerating very fast (for a ship). Cruising speed was only half that, but could be maintained all day. As the galley's main weapon in the classical period was its bronze ram, a favourite Athenian tactic was to shoot alongside an enemy trireme (shipping oars on the exposed side) so that the ram on the Athenian trireme's bow broke off all the enemy's oars, crippling it. Another tactic was to pass the enemy and then execute a rapid turn, ramming the enemy in his vulnerable stern. A development, perfected by the Rhodians, the finest Greek sailors after 322BC, was to dig in the front oars so that their prow dipped and their ram hit the enemy beneath the waterline, his most vulnerable point.

All such tactics required truly professional crews. Only Athens, which had about 350 triremes in its standing fleet by 431BC, could normally maintain these. Later, when Alexander's successors built huge fleets of massive vessels, galleys became primarily floating platforms for catapults and marines.

Above: A dramatic vision of a trireme at full tilt under sail and oars. The oarsmen were tiered above each other.

THE *OLYMPIAS*

In 1987 the first trireme since antiquity was launched in Greece, the *Olympias* (named after Alexander the Great's mother), commissioned into the Greek navy. The successful construction, launch and sailing of this galley answered some of the questions that have plagued historians – for example, all oars *were* the same length. But although rowed by fit young athletes from (mostly British) universities, it has not resolved all problems. It failed to reach the speeds expected, despite heroic efforts by its oarsmen. Major communication problems were solved only by electrically piping orders to the lower tiers. (This being impossible in ancient Greece, there must have been other ways of relaying commands.) Further, the 170 modern rowers could keep time only by singing together, and this is almost certainly *not* how the Greeks kept time. The ship's trierarch could never have given orders if everyone was singing. Also, the lower tiers of *Olympias'* rowers became so thirsty that they drank all the water on board and more had to be brought in. This suggests that, splendid though the *Olympias* is, it is not the full solution to the trireme question.

Above: The Olympias, *the only recreation of an ancient galley ever built or sailed. How accurate it is remains disputed, for it proved slow and exhaustingly heavy to row for any time.*

CATAPULTS AND SIEGE TOWERS
MASSIVE MACHINERY

Above: Demetrius I, king of Macedonia 317–288BC, gained the title Poliorcetes (besieger) for his huge siege towers that rose to seven floors. But even with such giants he proved unable to capture the city of Rhodes, abandoning his towers after a long siege in 304BC.

Below: Soldiers attacking a city. (These scenes comes from the Nereid funerary monument, hence their nakedness. Greek soldiers always wore body armour while fighting.)

Until the discovery of gunpowder in the 14th century AD, catapults were the most powerful weapons any army could field. (Catapult is in origin a Greek word meaning to hurl down.) But as ways of capturing cities they were surpassed by siege towers, which in the 4th century BC, became gigantic, fundamentally altering the relationship between attacker and defender in sieges. From then on, no city could regard itself as impregnable. Although the Assyrians had used catapults in the 7th century BC, their true pioneer was Dionysius I of Syracuse, who established war laboratories for his great attack on the Carthaginians in 397BC.

NON-TORSION CATAPULTS
Two types of catapult were used: non-torsion and torsion. The first was like a far stronger hand-held bow that needed drawing back by muscle power or ratchets. The early ones were just scaled-up crossbows called *gastraphetes* (literally 'stomach bows', as the butt of the bow rested in the stomach), with trigger mechanisms. There were obvious limits as to how far even the strongest men could draw these by muscle power. But, when set on a stand and using a winch to draw the string, huge composite bows (made of horn, wood and sinew) could be very powerful. They could fire bolts – even two simultaneously – for 182m/200 yards, out-ranging normal bows.

Such catapults, mounted on siege towers, would keep defenders cowering behind their walls, as happened at Motya in Sicily. But defenders could also install catapults on walls to shoot down besiegers, as occurred during Alexander's epic siege of Tyre in 332BC. Onomarchus of Phocis had used non-torsion catapults to repulse Philip II in 354BC, an unusual defeat that taught Philip the value of these weapons. Other Macedonian rulers and later the Romans used these giant crossbows widely, the Romans deploying them even in the field. They remained expensive weapons, however. When King Archidamus II of Sparta saw one, he was stunned, exclaiming: "By Hercules, now men's courage is a thing of the past!"

TORSION CATAPULTS
Philip's great engineer Polyeidus of Thessaly developed true torsion catapults, probably only after 340BC when Philip had signally failed to capture the cities of Byzantium and Selymbria. These catapults derived their power from twisted springs (*tonoi*) made of animal sinew, hair or similarly resilient material. Their potential was much greater and they could fire heavier bolts or stones, reputedly weighing up to 82kg/180lb, at least twice as far as non-torsion catapults.

Such weapons could be used to smash down walls and buildings and lob flaming material into cities. Alexander first used them to devastating effect when attacking Halicarnassus in 334BC, and again at Tyre

ARCHIMEDES' INVENTIONS

Syracuse, the greatest Greek city in the west, had allied itself with Rome under Hieron II of Syracuse (ruled 265–215BC) and prospered greatly. But his successors unwisely repudiated the alliance after Hannibal's third annihilatory victory at Cannae. The Romans, alarmed, sent an army under Marcellus to capture the city.

Syracuse's formidable walls were backed up by other, more remarkable wonder weapons devised by its most illustrious resident: the mathematician and scientist Archimedes (287–212BC). When Roman quinqueremes tried to attack Syracuse on its seaward side by acting as floating siege towers, some being lashed together, a hail of missiles from catapults firing through slits forced them to retreat. Later, a Roman night attack was countered by giant cranes concealed behind the walls swinging out to drop huge stones on the Roman galleys or to grab them by their prows and so sink them. Marcellus finally had to capture the city by stealth, which was not the preferred Roman way.

Above: A Roman soldier, discovering but not recognizing Archimedes at work during the fall of Syracuse, killed him – against the orders of Marcellus, the Roman commander. Archimedes' innovatory strengthening of Syracuse's defences had made the city almost impregnable.

A DOUBLE-EDGED WEAPON

Elephants were a double-edged weapon. If terrifying charging en masse, they were prone to run amok and do as much damage to their own side as the enemy in battle. Further, ways were soon found to counter them. At the siege of Mantinea in 312BC spikes concealed under the earth by the city's defenders penetrated the beasts' soft feet to devastating effect. In reality, elephants were more prestigious than effective. In the last great battle when they were used, when the Seleucid army faced the Romans at Magnesia in 190BC, they hurt the Romans less than the Macedonians. Soon after, the Romans hamstrung the Seleucid elephants in their stud farm, ending the Seleucids' supply.

Right: After Seleucus I acquired 500 elephants in return for ceding his Indian lands, elephants became seen as super-weapons. In fact, although en masse they were formidable, they were hard to control in battle and could easily turn against friendly troops.

CHAPTER VI

FROM ALEXANDER TO HADRIAN

323BC–AD138

Alexander's sudden death without a proper heir plunged his empire into chaos. It also ended his dream of Perso-Macedonian unity. The large kingdoms that emerged from the Wars of the Diadochi (successors) are called Hellenistic, because they were essentially Hellenic (Greek) in culture and politics. But their rulers were Macedonians. Although few of these kingdoms lasted very long, Greek culture was everywhere triumphant, reaching even into India. Luxury and magnificence, epitomized by the huge statue of the Colossus of Rhodes, marked the age. Trade boomed across this wide new world, while women enjoyed greater freedom. In the end, most of it fell to the relentlessly expanding power of Rome.

One woman embodies the age and its passing: Cleopatra VII, last Hellenistic queen of Egypt. With her death in 30BC the Romans controlled the Greek world, which they had half-wrecked with their wars. The *pax Romana*, the long Roman peace that followed, allowed Greek cities to recover, while the Romans adopted and spread Greek culture. This process reached its climax under the philhellenic Hadrian (AD117–138).

Left: The Colossus of Rhodes, *a huge statue of the sun god which collapsed, painted by Louis de Caulery* c.*1580-1622.*

THE WARS OF THE SUCCESSORS 323–275BC

Above: Coin showing Ptolemy I, one of Alexander's generals and the first Ptolemaic king of Egypt (322–283BC). He was the ancestor of Cleopatra VII, the last and most famous Ptolemaic queen.

Below: Seleucus I, founder of the Seleucid Empire that at times stretched from the Aegean to the Hindu Kush. Seleucus had an Iranian wife, so all later Seleucid kings had some Persian genes.

Asked on his deathbed in June 323BC who should be his heir, Alexander reputedly said: "the strongest". This proved prophetic, for he had scarcely stopped breathing before his generals began fighting to control the empire. There were, however, two possible heirs of Macedonian royal blood, to whom the army turned: Alexander's idiot half-brother Arrhidaeus (who became Philip III on succeeding to the throne) and Roxane's son, Alexander IV, born in September. If Hephaistion, Grand Vizier and Alexander's oldest friend, had lived, the latter especially might have survived. As it was, the two simply became pawns of the warring generals (the Diadochi).

At first all the contestants paid lip service to the concept of an empire united under the joint kings, who reigned over rather than ruled the empire. Three men initially appeared to dominate the scene: Perdiccas, Alexander's second-in-command; Antipater, the old general left as viceroy of Macedonia, and Craterus, commanding the discharged Macedonian veterans. Perdiccas, acting as regent in Babylon, read out what he claimed was Alexander's will to the army. This included megalomaniac plans for war against Carthage, gigantic temples and massive transfers of population between Europe and Asia. Proving as unacceptable as intended, it was unanimously rejected.

Ptolemy, one of Alexander's boyhood friends, was made governor of Egypt, to which he added Cyrene (east Libya). Antipater, crushing the Greek states in the Lamian War in 322BC, became guardian of the young kings, establishing a Macedonian power base that he left to his son Cassander on his death. In central Asia a revolt by unhappy colonists who wanted to return home was quelled. Antigonus I, governor of Phrygia (central Asia Minor), now began extending his power south. By 316BC he had emerged as the strongest single ruler with the aid of his son Demetrius. But endless wars prevented him gaining more than western Asia, despite brilliant sieges by Demetrius, who built giant siege towers to attack Cyprus and Rhodes. Meanwhile Lysimachus carved out a kingdom in Thrace and northern Asia Minor.

THE RISE OF SELEUCUS

In 312BC Seleucus, once Alexander's infantry commander, became governor of Babylon and all lands eastward. After one of the joint kings, Alexander IV, the last of Alexander's family, was murdered by Cassander in 311BC, Antigonus took the title of king, later followed by Ptolemy and Seleucus.

In 303BC Seleucus ceded his Indian provinces to King Chandragupta Maurya in return for 500 war elephants, a huge force. Allied with Lysimachus, he used this to defeat and kill Antigonus at the Battle of Ipsus in 301BC (there were 75,000 troops on either side), gaining the title *Nicator* (victor). In all these conflicts, Macedonian soldiers remained remarkably loyal to their generals, while native populations suffered in silence the passage of the warlords with their armies. Whether their rulers were Macedonian or Persian hardly worried them.

By eliminating the only potential reunifier of Alexander's empire, the Battle of Ipsus led to the emergence of four distinct kingdoms: Ptolemy I firmly controlling Egypt and southern Syria;

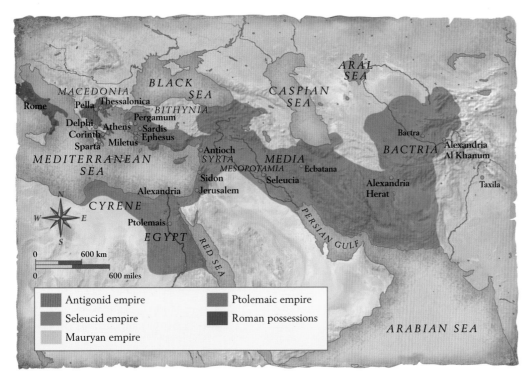

Left: Alexander's successors divided up his huge empire into constantly warring kingdoms of markedly unequal size.

Cassander shakily ruling Macedonia and parts of Greece; Lysimachus expanding his power in Thrace and Asia Minor; and Seleucus with a huge empire stretching from the Aegean to central Asia. Lysimachus' expansionism led to the next war. When in 281BC Lysimachus was defeated and killed by Seleucus, his kingdom collapsed completely. In contrast, after Seleucus' own murder in 280BC, his son Antiochus I succeeded him smoothly, ruling from the new capital of Antioch in north Syria.

Meanwhile the *poleis* (citizen-states) of Greece itself, dominated by Macedonia, periodically regained or lost their freedom. Macedonia installed garrisons at the four 'chains of Greece': Corinth, Piraeus, Chalcis in Euboea and Demetrias in Thessaly. Macedonia normally favoured oligarchies, but the distinction between democracy and oligarchy was growing blurred. All the old citizen-states were hugely outgunned by the new kingdoms.

ARRIVAL OF THE GAULS

No one was prepared for the impact of the Gauls, however. These wild Celtic invaders burst into Greece *c.*280BC, even threatening Delphi, the holiest shrine in Greece. Antigonus II, king of Macedonia and grandson of both Antipater and Antigonus I, triumphantly repelled them in 278BC, consolidating his position and earning some Greek gratitude.

The Gauls, crossing into Asia, were defeated by the Seleucid Antiochus I in 275BC. They were permitted to settle in central Asia Minor in the land called subsequently Galatia after them.

THE BALANCE OF POWER

These battles confirmed the new balance of power. Much the richest and most stable kingdom was that of the Ptolemies, based in Egypt but extending its power into Syria and the Aegean islands. If much the smallest kingdom, Macedonia, had excellent soldiers and the prestige of the old Macedonian crown, while the huge realm of the Seleucids at times tempted its monarchs with the (unrealizable) prospect of recreating Alexander's whole empire.

War, however, was the norm between the kingdoms and frontiers remained very fluid.

Below: The winged Nike (victory) of Samothrace, one of the finest Hellenistic statues, was probably commissioned to celebrate a victory by Antigonus II, king of Macedonia, in c.250BC.

THE GREEK PHARAOHS
PTOLEMAIC EGYPT, 322–200 BC

Above: Alexandria's most famous symbol was its pharos *(lighthouse), the light of which could be seen 50km/32 miles off, as depicted on a 2nd century AD Roman coin.*

Below: The tombs of Anfouchy of the 3rd century BC are among the few structures of the Ptolemaic era to survive. (Most are under water or have been destroyed.) The tombs reveal mixed Greek and Egyptian influence in the burial of the dead.

Ptolemy had noticed the potential of Egypt when Alexander annexed it in 332BC. The richest satrapy in Persia's empire after Babylonia, Egypt was unusual in being a distinct nation, defensible behind its deserts. When Ptolemy obtained its governorship in 322BC, he covertly began creating a separate state, annexing Cyrene. Kidnapping Alexander's embalmed corpse when it was en route to Macedonia, Ptolemy finally installed it at the new capital Alexandria in a grand mausoleum that also held the Ptolemies' tombs. He defeated and killed Perdiccas, who had attacked him for this act. (Perdiccas' men were reputedly devoured by Nile crocodiles after the battle.)

Ptolemy founded only one new city, Ptolemais, in the south, for the bulk of the population remained Egyptian *fellahin* (peasants). To them, the Ptolemies were pharaohs, god-kings, hailed by the priesthood, who initially welcomed them after Persian misrule. The Ptolemies tried to

THE PTOLEMAIA
In the winter of 275–274BC a huge festival, the Ptolemaia, was staged in Alexandria to celebrate both the dynasty and its patron deity Dionysus, god of wine and theatre. Great floats processed along the Canopic Way. They carried wild animals, including a white bear; a huge winepress worked by men dressed as satyrs dispensing 114,000 litres/25,000 gallons of wine; women dressed as maenads, the god's ecstatic followers; a pole 55m/180ft high representing a gigantic phallus; models of the morning and evening star; and, in the rear, 57,000 marching soldiers.

impress their subjects by restoring temples damaged by the Persians and building new ones in the time-hallowed style, such as that at Edfu begun in 237BC. But no Ptolemy before Cleopatra VII (51–30BC) ever learned Egyptian. They relied instead on Greek or Macedonian administrators and *cleruchs* (Macedonian military colonists who received grants of land). When Ptolemy I died – in bed, unlike most Successors – in 283BC, he was succeeded by his son Ptolemy II (283–246BC). This cultured monarch married his sister Arsinoe, reviving the old Egyptian custom. More dynamic than her husband, Arsinoe effectively ruled Egypt until her death in 270BC.

GOLDEN AGE
The 3rd century BC was the Ptolemies' Golden Age. Ptolemy II's chief minister Apollonius perfected the fullest state bureaucracy yet seen, regulating every aspect of life. The marsh of the Fayum was reclaimed and Greek officials introduced new crops, including vines and olives. But Egypt's staple product

Above: Egypt, unlike most Persian satrapies, had had a strong national identity since the time when the first pyramids were built.

remained grain, grown by serfs tied to the land who owned nothing, not even their seed corn. All products were either heavily taxed or royal monopolies like papyrus, the precursor of paper. The resulting wealth flowed down the Nile into the royal treasury, enabling the Ptolemies to maintain huge fleets and armies. Crete, Cyprus, Samos, Cilicia and southern Syria became part of their empire, although the last was disputed by the Seleucid kings in the Syrian Wars.

ALEXANDRIA THE COSMOPOLIS

The fruits of this systematic tax-gathering were enjoyed in Alexandria, the world's first cosmopolis, welcoming Greek and other immigrants, including many Jews. With its double harbour and *pharos* – the lighthouse rising 90m/300ft, with colossal statues of a Ptolemy and his queen as pharaohs at its base – the city became the greatest in the Mediterranean. Its population probably passed 500,000 by 200BC. Its trade eclipsed that of Athens or Carthage, reaching down the Red Sea to India by 116BC. The Canopic Way, an avenue 45m/150ft wide lined with colonnades, ran west from the Gate of the Sun through the city, intersecting with similarly grand boulevards. In the west stood the Library-cum-Museum (the world's largest such building, with 500,000 scrolls, which became Hellenism's intellectual

powerhouse); a great temple to Sarapis; and an artificial hill dedicated to the god Pan. In the east royal palaces were grouped round parks, with fleets of luxurious royal pleasure barges. Beyond them stood the Hippodrome for chariot races and the Gymnasium, an important institution in Hellenistic life where men met to socialize as much as to exercise.

Alexandria was never regarded as part of Egypt proper. While it had a council of some sort, it was never a *polis* in the full Greek sense either. But Greek was the official language spoken by everyone of importance, although many races at first rubbed shoulders amiably enough.

The splendour of Alexandria depended finally on the overworked *fellahin*, for long ignored except as serfs. But in 217BC Antiochus III invaded from Syria. To repel him, Ptolemy IV conscripted Egyptian peasants en masse into the army. The resulting Egyptian victory at Raphia repelled the Seleucids for a time but revealed the growing weakness of the dynasty. Riots, strikes and rebellions began to appear in the 2nd century BC, as an increasingly corrupt bureaucracy oppressed ordinary Egyptians.

Above: Alexandria, the great port, was Ptolemy's chosen capital, replacing inland cities such as Memphis.

Below: The pylon (gateway) of the Temple of Horus at Edfu. Begun in 237BC, it exactly replicates the styles of earlier temples, for the Ptolemies posed as pharaohs to their Egyptian subjects.

SARDIS TO SAMARKAND
THE SELEUCID EMPIRE, 312–200 BC

Above: A coin of Antiochus III the Great (reigned 223–187BC), who restored Seleucid power across Asia. He took southern Syria from Egypt before finally being defeated by Rome.

Below: Perge was one of the many Greek cities in Asia Minor that frequently accepted Seleucid suzerainty while keeping its internal autonomy.

More than any other successors, the Seleucids earned the right to call themselves Alexander's heirs, since they were the greatest disseminators of Greek civilization. At its peak in 280BC their empire stretched from the Aegean, where Sardis was the regional capital, to Samarcand in central Asia, an area of 3,885,000 sq km/1,500,000 square miles. It had a population of *c*.30 million – five times more than Egypt's.

To control this huge realm, Seleucus I and his son Antiochus I (281–261BC) continued Alexander's policy of founding cities at strategic points on a grand scale. (Seleucus alone reputedly founded 50). These were settled mostly with retired Macedonian troops who often married local women, their descendants later becoming full citizens. From them the Seleucids could recruit fresh generations of troops.

SELEUCIA DISPLACES BABYLON
Most new cities were called Antioch, Seleucia, Laodicea (after Seleucus I's mother) or Apamea (after Apama, his Persian wife and mother of Antiochus I). Alone of Alexander's successors, Seleucus did not repudiate his Persian wife and employed some Iranians, although the culture and politics of his new empire were Hellenistic. Seleucus I, by 312BC ruling Babylonia and eastern satrapies, founded Seleucia-on-the-Tigris on the site of Opis (now Baghdad), where a canal linked the two rivers and Alexander had once prayed for Perso-Macedonian harmony. It rapidly grew to displace Babylon as the commercial metropolis of western Asia, and Babylon fell into decay.

Seleucia's population – 600,000 in the 1st century BC, according to the geographer Strabo – remained proudly Greek, with a council, elected officials and assembly. It included people of Babylonian ancestry among its citizens.

Nearly every Seleucid foundation resembled a Greek *polis*, at least internally. Like the Romans later, the Seleucids saw their empire as a confederation of cities, to which they granted autonomy and land, sometimes with seed corn and equipment. In return, the cities were generally loyal to the dynasty, often hailing its kings as gods.

ANTIOCH THE CAPITAL
The main Seleucid capital was Antioch-on-the-Orontes in northern Syria, only 24km/15 miles from the Mediterranean, which was important to the sea-loving Greeks. Founded in 300BC, Antioch soon rivalled Alexandria in splendour and sophistication. It became the terminus for caravan routes across Asia, taxes on trade being vital to Seleucid revenues. Antioch was peopled initially with Macedonian and Athenian colonists, but many Jews

settled there later. Near Antioch the Seleucids established a stud farm to breed their renowned Indian war elephants, a pillar of their power. (Another pillar was the standing army, *c.*70,000 strong, the biggest yet seen.) The kings founded so many cities in northern Syria along the fertile Orontes valley that it resembled a second Macedonia. It was one of the few parts of Asia to be so fully Hellenized, though Phoenicia and parts of Mesopotamia were also lightly settled with Greek cities.

THE LOSS OF THE EAST

Further east, Greek cities were mere outposts of Hellenism amid an unchanged rural population. Few Iranian nobles adopted Greek customs. Generally, Graeco-Macedonian settlers' ingrained contempt for 'barbarians' doomed Seleucid attempts at mass Hellenization.

The Seleucid Empire from the start contained several types of state. Most manageable were city-states the kings themselves had founded – or, in the Aegean and Phoenicia, conquered – whose autonomy they normally respected. Far older were priestly temple-states, whose power and prestige the kings tried to curb while respecting their religious role and immunity from taxation. In Babylonia, the most civilized and richest part of their empire, the Seleucids attempted with some success to win the support of priests and merchants.

However, on the Iranian plateau, heartland of the Achaemenid Empire, they had less impact. The Seleucids had to rely on powerful satraps, or governors, who in turn depended partly on still feudal Persian nobles, who ruled their estates from their castles. The huge distances from the Seleucid heartland of Syria-Babylonia usually prevented effective royal control.

Around 255BC Diodotus, governor of Bactria, revolted against Antiochus II (ruled 261–246BC) and the huge province was lost to the empire, permanently as it turned out. But at least Diodotus was

Right: A bust of an unknown philosopher, one of the many Greeks attracted to the new cities that the Seleucids founded across their huge empire, which had all the trappings of a polis: *agora, gymnasium, stoa, theatre.*

Macedonian. In 247BC, Arsaces, king of the Parthians, an Iranian people, broke away from Diodotus, and his successors began expanding his kingdom in central Iran. In the 2nd century BC the Parthians over-ran ever more Seleucid territories, finally capturing Babylonia by 130BC.

To restore Seleucid power, Antiochus III made a grand military expedition through the east in 212–206BC. He forced rebel governors to recognize his suzerainty but accepted Bactria's independence, despite defeating it. He began calling himself Great King, like the Persians, but such triumphalism proved premature. Soon after he returned, the remoter satraps reasserted their independence. No later Seleucid ventured so far east. Seleucid power would soon face a new enemy: Rome.

Below: Ephesus, as the Aegean terminus of the transasiatic trade routes, flourished anew under the Seleucids, whose westernmost capital it sometimes was. These houses date from c.300BC.

MACEDONIA AND PERGAMUM
HELLENISTIC POWERS

0From Macedonia, a country large only by the standards of classical Greece, came the armies that had conquered half of Asia and most of the colonists needed to establish the new Hellenistic cities. But even this combined effort did not exhaust the kingdom. It remained one of the key players in the eastern Mediterranean until Rome finally ended its existence in 168BC. Its army and navy, if relatively small, were very fine, while its much-contested control of Greece gave it both prestige and power. Macedonia itself became increasingly wealthy and fully Hellenized in the 3rd century BC. The *koine*, the common Greek dialect based on Attic (Athenian), replaced the old Macedonian dialect, as it did across the Hellenistic world.

Cassander, son of Alexander the Great's old regent Antipater, killed the boy-king Alexander IV, last of the old royal house, in 311BC. He founded the great city of Thessalonica and ruled Macedonia until his death in 297BC. Demetrius I 'the Besieger' then briefly regained control of Macedonia and Greece, but lost both when Pyrrhus of Epirus invaded from the west and Lysimachus attacked from the east. For a moment Macedonia's very existence seemed threatened until Demetrius' son – and Antipater's grandson, for the successors intermarried – Antigonus II (284–239BC) won the throne.

ANTIGONUS AND HIS SUCCESSORS
Beating the invading Gauls decisively at Lysimachia in 278BC, Antigonus reasserted Macedonia's role as a major power and ensured the future of his dynasty. He defeated the Spartans and Athenians in the Chremonidean War (267–262BC), reasserting Macedonian hegemony over Greece through the four strategic forts called the 'chains'. But he treated the Athenians tactfully. In alliance with the Seleucids, he also repulsed the Egyptian navy off Cos and Andros, checking Ptolemaic expansion in the Aegean. Antigonus encouraged Macedonia's agriculture and trade, drawing most of his revenue from his own estates without taxing his people heavily, despite extensive use of mercenaries. Private houses excavated at Pella and Thessalonica reveal Macedonian wealth and sophistication at this time.

Antigonus' successor, his son Demetrius II, was killed in 229BC fighting northern barbarians – Macedonia long acted as a breakwater against such invaders. He was succeeded in turn by his son Philip V in 221BC after a regency. Philip was handsome, energetic and ambitious. Hailed as a saviour of Greece at the Conference of Naupactus in 217BC, which attempted to find a lasting peace,

Above: The fortifications of Acrocorinth high above the port, one of the 'chains of Greece' or garrisoned citadels with which the Macedonian kings controlled Greece.

Below: The dramatically sited theatre at Pergamum (Asia Minor) proclaimed the power and wealth of the Attalid dynasty, at its peak in the 2nd century BC.

two years later he fatally allied himself with Carthage against Rome. Hannibal, its great general, appeared to be winning the Second Punic War (218–202BC). This led to the First Macedonian War. A Roman force landed in north-west Greece, did some desultory fighting and made an alliance with the Aetolian League in central Greece. Peace was made on a return to the *status quo ante* in 205BC, but Rome's suspicious attention had now been turned on Macedonia.

THE RISE OF PERGAMUM

Pergamum, a previously obscure hill town in north-west Asia Minor commanding the fertile Caicus valley, became one of the great Hellenistic powers under its Attalid rulers. Its rise began in 263BC when its governor, Eumenes I, broke away. Although the Seleucids forced him to disgorge most territorial gains, he remained independent. After his successor Attalus I (241–197BC) won a dramatic victory over the Gauls, he assumed a crown and the title *Soter* (saviour) of Hellenism.

Attalus began looking west, cultivating Rome's friendship by reporting the (allegedly) dangerous ambitions of Philip V of Macedonia and the Seleucids. His son Eumenes II (197–160BC) continued this pro-Roman policy. Crucially, Eumenes supported the Romans at the Battle of Magnesia in 190BC.

Gaining a huge slice of territory in Asia Minor in return for this help, Eumenes II made Pergamum one of the architectural and artistic marvels of the Hellenistic world. Its temples and theatres rose dramatically up its hillside, while its library rivalled Alexandria's. The melodramatic splendour of the Pergamum Altar epitomizes the kingdom's flamboyant wealth. To challenge Egypt's monopoly of papyrus, parchment was reputedly invented at Pergamum, from which comes its name. Royal herds of cattle and flocks of sheep produced the hides needed for this tough, enduring writing material. In its autocratic bureaucracy, Pergamum resembled Egypt more closely

than the Seleucid realm, with many peasants working for the crown as serfs. Although the kings treated the old Ionian cities that came under their control after 189BC with diplomatic restraint, most Greeks could never forget that Attalid wealth and power stemmed from craven collaboration with Rome.

Above: The Pergamum Altar, *one of the grandest and most flamboyant in the Greek world, expresses the wealth of the Attalid kingdom of Pergamum at its 2nd-century peak. It is now in Berlin.*

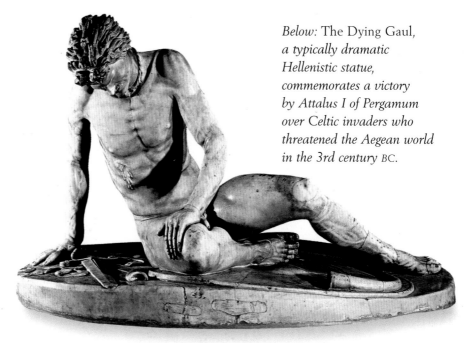

Below: The Dying Gaul, a typically dramatic Hellenistic statue, commemorates a victory by Attalus I of Pergamum over Celtic invaders who threatened the Aegean world in the 3rd century BC.

THE GREEKS IN THE EAST
BACTRIA AND INDIA, 350–320BC

Above: Antimachus I, Hellenistic king of Bactria (Afghanistan), conquered north-western India in c.180BC, minting fine coins such as this.

Below: Eucratides I, king of Bactria c.170–155BC, ruled a huge Indo-Greek kingdom stretching from Merv in Central Asia to Taxila in northern India.

Alexander had founded cities in Bactria (Afghanistan), Sogdiana (Tadzhikstan) and in north-western India (Pakistan) primarily for military purposes. Their often unwillingly retired soldiers would, he intended, safeguard strategically important routes and provide fresh recruits in their sons, whose mothers would be local women. Or at least that was the idea. But 20,000 settlers revolted even before Alexander's death, returning to their colonies only under compulsion from Macedonian generals

The Seleucids continued Alexander's colonization policy but on a wider, and generally much sounder, basis. They re-established some cities and founded many further ones (often named Antioch) but made each a proper Greek *polis* with a proper council, assembly, theatre and gymnasium.

ARTISTIC FUSION

Whether or not Menander converted to Buddhism, the fusion of Greek aesthetic form with Buddhist religious ideas proved hugely influential. Chinese and even Japanese art echoes Hellenic forms, while the huge Buddhas of Bamiyan, dating from c.AD500, showed traces of Greek art. The intellectual impact proved long-lasting, too. The *Gorgi Samhita*, an astronomical work of AD230, states: "Although the Yavanas (Ionians, i.e. Greeks) are barbarians, the science of astronomy originated with them, for which they should be revered like gods."

THE RUINS OF AI KHANUM

These cities retained their Hellenic identity for a remarkably long time, as the ruins of Ai Khanum show. Originally Alexandria-on-the-Oxus in Bactria, perhaps refounded by Seleucus I, it is sited in what was then a fertile area. The ruins include a huge gymnasium, a big terraced theatre near the river, large private houses and a palace with ornate Corinthian columns around a grand courtyard. Around 300BC Clearchus, a pupil of Aristotle, brought from distant Delphi the traditional maxims for the Five Ages of Man (as the Greeks numbered them) to be inscribed in this gymnasium. A papyrus with scraps of Aristotle's philosophy has been unearthed nearby, suggesting that Greek citizens of this central Asian *polis* discussed philosophy after exercising in the gymnasium. The city reached its peak c.200BC.

THE GRAECO-BACTRIAN STATE

In 255BC Diodotus I, the Seleucid governor of Bactria, declared himself independent – perhaps despairing of

Above: Elephants, the 'tanks of ancient warfare', came mostly from India, where Alexander had encountered them in numbers at the Battle of the Hydaspes.

effective help from the Seleucids against nomadic invaders – and founded the Graeco-Bactrian state. His son Diodotus II (248–235BC) took a royal title and negotiated with the Parthians, now also independent, before being overthrown by Euthydemus I (235–200BC). An energetic king, Euthydemus retook Herat from the Parthians in the west, while in the northeast he penetrated into Sinkiang, now in China. Antiochus III defeated him but had to accept him as a subordinate ruler in 210BC. Most of what we know of these monarchs comes from their fine coinage, for there are few written records.

THE INDO-GREEKS

Seleucus I had ceded his eastern provinces to the first Maurya ruler Chandragupta in return for (reputedly) 500 elephants in 303BC. He acknowledged the rise of this new power in India by marrying one of his family to a Maurya. Although this had little political effect, it helped with Greek cultural diffusion, to which India proved very receptive. Chandragupta's grandson Asoka, possibly part-Greek by birth, became the first Buddhist emperor (274–232BC). He had

Buddhist decrees inscribed in Greek on pillars in Kandahar, showing the importance he attached both to his new pacifist religion and to his Greek-speaking subjects. He also employed Greek craftsmen.

DEMETRIUS AND HIS HEIRS

In the early 2nd century BC, with Maurya power declining, the Graeco-Bactrian monarchs began to regain lost territory and move east. Euthydemus' son Demetrius I (200–185BC) retook some Mauryan lands, founding a colony, Demetrias, near Ghazni. His kingdom was divided between three heirs. One, Antimachus I, controlled all of what is now northern Pakistan, minting resplendent coins. His successors ruled from Taxila, minting bilingual coins in Greek and Brahmi, the script of the Ganges valley. Another Indo-Greek monarch Demetrius Aniketos (Unconquered) issued coins in Greek and Prakrit. Increasingly, these coins began to bear Indian emblems, such as Lashkmi, the Hindu goddess, or a sacred tree, among Buddhism's holiest symbols. Some were even square, the preferred shape in Indian bazaars. In India the Greeks proved receptive to local culture, dropping their usual chauvinism.

Eucratides I (c.170–155BC), who took the Indian title Maharajasa (great king), ruled a united Indo-Greek kingdom from Merv in central Asia to Taxila. His successor, Menander (155–130BC), extended his power far east down the Ganges valley, his troops reaching Patna. His gold and silver coins have been found over a huge area, although he did not rule it all. He may, however, have converted to Buddhism, for he figures in Buddhist legends as Milinda the Just. Menander was succeeded by further Indo-Greek rulers, among them Queen Agathocleia, who ruled in her own right. But in the 1st century BC Scythian tribes, the Kushans, invaded Bactria and then north-western India, overthrowing the last Indo-Greek kingdom by 30BC.

Below: While all the Indo-Greek kingdoms had vanished by 30BC, Greek artistic influence persisted for centuries. It shaped depictions of the Buddha, as this Bodhisattva of Gandhara of the 4th century AD reveals.

OLD GREECE: THE AETOLIAN AND ACHAEAN LEAGUES, 320–180BC

Above: Ruins of the Tholos, Sanctuary, Athena Pronala, Delphi, control of which site signified control of old Greece.

Although Macedonian kings dominated old Greece after 322BC, garrisoning key points, Greek political – and economic and social – life was not dead. However, many smaller cities, while still cherishing their beloved autonomy, realized that they now had to band together in leagues to survive. In doing so, they showed continued Greek ingenuity and innovation until the steamroller of Roman conquest squashed all independence.

THE AETOLIAN LEAGUE

Isocrates, the 4th-century BC propagandist, had long called for Panhellenic union against 'barbarians'. Around 367BC, in the mountainous backwoods of Aetolia, many villages or cantons actually formed such a defensive league. This developed a remarkably flexible and inventive constitution, with a president and commander-in-chief annually elected who could not be re-elected on successive years. Other officials included a cavalry leader, secretary and seven financial stewards.

The League Assembly held two regular meetings a year, before and after the campaigning season, at the hilltop temple of Apollo at Thermum. Every adult male citizen had a vote and there was a federal *boule* (council) with 1,000 delegates. Each state was represented according to its population while retaining internal autonomy. Much business was later delegated to a committee of 40, for the League became less democratic as it grew. Policy remained in Aetolian hands, although some new states became honorary Aetolians.

The Aetolian League showed its strength after Alexander's death. Although its army was only 12,000 strong, it captured Naupactus on the Gulf of Corinth, repelling attacks by the Diadochi. By c.300BC it had gained control of Delphi. Although Delphi was never part of the League, the Aetolians justified their hold on the great shrine by defeating the Gauls in 279BC. In 245BC the Aetolians crushed the Boeotians, extending their power across central Greece. They generally opposed the Macedonians, posing as defenders of Greek liberty, but were also notoriously friendly to pirates.

Allied with Rome, they fought in the Second Macedonian War (200–197BC), their cavalry playing a decisive role in Roman victory at Cynoscephalae. Then, feeling that Rome had ignored them in the subsequent peace, they rashly invited the Seleucid Antiochus III into Greece in 192BC. After his defeat in 189BC, the League was reduced to Aetolia and became dependent on Rome, which later broke it up.

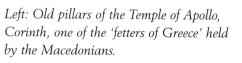

Left: Old pillars of the Temple of Apollo, Corinth, one of the 'fetters of Greece' held by the Macedonians.

Left: This painting by Victorian artist and humourist Edward Lear shows the narrow pass of Thermopylae. This, which always remained key to the control of Greece proper, for the 'Hot Gates' controlled access to central Greece from the north.

Below: This graceful terracotta figure comes from Tanagra in Boeotia, one of the numerous tiny cities that made up the powerful Aetolian League.

THE ACHAEAN LEAGUE

Equally significant was the Achaean League, which emerged c.280BC on the Peloponnese's north-west coast. Originally composed of ten coastal cities, by 251BC it included Sicyon near Corinth, which was not actually in Achaea. From Sicyon came Aratus, who for a generation headed the League as president and commander-in-chief, being re-elected every other year. The League's constitution emulated the Aetolians' but with differences. Only citizens over the age of 30 could vote in the *synedos*, or Council, which made it more conservative than the Assembly. Both met four times a year at Aigion on the Gulf, once to elect League officials such as the *hipparchs* (the cavalry commanders). Votes were taken by city, not head, to stop locals swamping the vote, but only richer citizens could afford to travel to Aigion. Each city retained its internal autonomy and coinage but followed League foreign policy.

Aratus, a passionate League patriot if no great general, pursued an anti-Macedonian policy. In 243BC he surprised the Macedonian garrison of Corinth by a night attack, adding that great port to the League. Over the next years, as Macedonia faced northern invasions, the League grew to include Argos, Megalopolis and finally almost all the Peloponnese except Sparta. These new citizens were all willing League members. But the League faced a resurgent Sparta after the reforms of Cleomones III, who captured city after city by appealing to the poor. Aratus was forced to call in the Macedonians to defeat the Spartans at Sellasia in 222BC. Under Philip V, however, the League's relations with Macedonia deteriorated and it turned to Rome. Philopoemon, its next great leader, accepted Roman help only very reluctantly. It was needed to defeat a resurgent Sparta again, which ultimately led to that proud city being enrolled in the League.

After Philopoemon's death from poisoning in Messenia in 182BC (Messenia had become another involuntary member) the Achaean League remained pro-Roman, but this did it no good at all. In 167BC, after the final defeat of Macedonia by Rome, 1,000 chiefly democratic Achaean hostages were taken to Rome, among them Polybius, the future historian. (Only 300 out of the 1,000 lived to return home.) Polybius himself came genuinely to admire Rome's unique constitution and wrote about Rome's rise to power. He also tried hard, if finally in vain, to persuade his country-men to accept increasingly stringent Roman demands.

ATHENS AND RHODES
323–170BC

Above: Athens, liberal and usually peaceful, still attracted the greatest philosophers such as Zeno of Citium, founder of Stoicism.

Below: The entrance to Rhodes Harbour, where the Colossus once stood.

Two cities dominated the Aegean in the Hellenistic period culturally and commercially: Athens and Rhodes. The former, still the greatest Greek city in 323BC, slowly ceded economic supremacy to Rhodes, the new mercantile power, but retained its cultural primacy. Rhodes became the wealthiest independent *polis* of the age and an unusually fine example of limited democracy. Both cities ultimately fell to Rome's imperialism despite their attempts to placate it.

ATHENS: GREECE'S INTELLECTUAL AND CULTURAL CAPITAL

The Lamian War of 323–322BC, when the Greek alliance was crushed by Macedonia, ended Athenian independence and full democracy. Cassander's protégé Demetrius of Phalerum's bizarre regime in Athens mixed philosophy, authoritarianism and sybaritism. When Demetrius I the Besieger ousted Cassander's men in 307BC, democracy was partly restored, although the Assembly was no longer supreme. Exploiting Macedonian weakness during the Gaulish invasions of 280BC, Athens regained full independence but lost it to Antigonus II of Macedonia in 262BC. Antigonus, while installing a garrison in Piraeus, treated Athens tactfully – he saw it as his cultural capital, as did increasingly many Greeks.

The city's economy revived thanks to new veins of silver found at the Laurium mines, and later its control of Delos' free port. In 229BC Athens managed to buy out the Macedonian garrison, becoming effectively neutral. It cultivated Rome's friendship in the 2nd century BC, long escaping the worst wars.

Athens' importance was now overwhelmingly intellectual and cultural. It remained, most of the time, a modified democracy and it became the definitive home of philosophy. Epicurus and Zeno of Citium founded their respective schools – Epicureanism and Stoicism – c.300BC in the city, alongside the existing Platonists and Aristotelians. At the same time, Menander started the New Comedy, the origin of all subsequent 'sit coms'. Non-political in content but psychologically astute, it influenced Roman writers such as Plautus.

Hellenistic kings competed to honour Athens with fine buildings. The Seleucid Antiochus IV in the 170s BC paid for work to be restarted on the gigantic Temple of Zeus abandoned 340 years earlier, although it was not completed until the Emperor Hadrian's reign three centuries later.

On the east of the Agora in 140BC Attalus II of Pergamum built the Stoa, a huge colonnade, the last and largest of many. Beneath such colonnades the philosopher Zeno taught (so his followers were named 'Stoics'). Stoas sheltered shoppers and other citizens too. Athens' Indian summer of prosperity lasted until after 100BC, when it rashly sided with Mithradates of Pontus against Rome.

Right: Many Hellenistic monarchs endowed Athens, still the supreme Hellenic polis, *with grand buildings. The Seleucid king Antiochus IV in 174BC paid for work to restart on the vast Temple of Olympian Zeus begun in the 6th century BC, but work had not gone far before Antiochus' murder cut off funds.*

RHODES: A MARITIME REPUBLIC

In 406BC Rhodes's three small cities united to form a single democratic *polis*. Ruled by outside powers in the 4th century BC, after Alexander's death Rhodes declared itself free and expelled its Macedonian garrison. When Demetrius I besieged it in 305–304BC with giant siege towers, it repelled him. Rhodes enjoyed a period of great prosperity down to 166BC, displacing Athens as the hub of the Aegean. Its wealth came from its superb position at the centre of trade routes to Sicily, the Black Sea and Egypt. In 170BC its two per cent carrying tariff, primarily on wheat, yielded a million drachmas. As a result, Rhodes became the Hellenistic world's banking centre.

Rhodian democracy was limited but its aristocracy had a strong sense of *noblesse oblige*, richer citizens helping the poorer. Because of this, Rhodes enjoyed unusual social stability. All citizens served in the fleet. This albeit small fleet, comprising about 50 galleys, mostly quinqueremes,

became the best in the Hellenistic world, again paid for by the rich. Rhodes suppressed piracy as Athens had once done, promulgating a maritime code later adopted by imperial Rome. When an earthquake shattered the city in 226BC, other Greek states combined to restore it, so central had Rhodes become to their political and commercial wellbeing.

Rhodes favoured a neutrality that protected its trade, but allied itself with Rome against Philip V and Antiochus III because it feared their ambitions. Its immediate reward was large: Lycia and Caria, former Seleucid territory in Asia Minor. But Rome, growing suspicious of *any* Greek state's true independence, thought it was too neutral in the Third Macedonian War (171–168BC) and made Delos a free port, so ruining Rhodes' trade. Rhodes remained culturally important, attracting poets such as Apollonius Rhodius in the 3rd century BC and philosophers such as Poseidonius (135–50BC). The future emperor Tiberius withdrew there in 6BC, actually in a sulk at being sidelined in the imperial succession but supposedly to study philosophy.

THE COLOSSUS OF RHODES

Symbol of Rhodes' maritime wealth and one of the Seven Wonders of the World, the famous *Colossus of Rhodes* according to legend straddled the harbour entrance. In reality it did not but was impressive enough: a bronze statue of the sun god 33m/110ft high. Falling in the earthquake of 226BC, even its mighty remnants long impressed visitors. The much-copied statue of snake-strangled Laocoön and his sons marked the Rhodian school of sculpture's zenith *c.*180BC, but the whole city was adorned with artworks.

Below: In Athens, the classical tradition in art continued, creating vivid new works such as this Maenad of c.100BC.

REVOLUTION IN SPARTA
244–192BC

Above: The Vix Crater *is an unusually fine example of Laconian craftmanship.*

Since Sparta's crushing defeat by Thebes in 371BC and subsequent loss of Messenia, it had been of only minor importance, even in Greece. Its falling birth rate, coupled with the concentration of land among ever fewer rich people, meant that there were fewer full Spartiates – only 700 by 300BC – to be the hoplites that still formed the army's core. Discontent among the disenfranchised, who had lost their lands and citizenship, threatened Spartan stability. Despite this, memories of Sparta's former hegemony remained potent among both its neighbours and rulers.

AGIS THE REVOLUTIONARY
In 244BC Agis IV became king, determined on a return to the legendary excellence of the 'Lycurgan' constitution. Agis planned to divide the land into 4,500 equal lots, cancel all mortgages, allow many Spartans to regain their citizenship and enfranchise some *perioeci* (second-class citizens). This horrified conservatives: the magistrates (*ephors*), his co-monarch Leonidas II and rich citizens. Agis drove Leonidas into exile and deposed some *ephors*, but when Leonidas returned in 241BC, Agis was killed.

CLEOMENES' REFORMS
In 235BC Cleomenes III became king. Although he was the son of Leonidas, listening to Agis' widow had made him a revolutionary. He was also inspired by the teachings of the Stoic philosopher Sphaerus. Realizing that force was needed to implement reform, Cleomenes drove through revolutionary changes. He abolished debt; nationalized the land, dividing it into 4,000 lots for Spartiates and 15,000 for *perioeci*; and boosted the number of Spartiates by promoting *perioeci* or even *helots* (serfs). He also sold 1,000 *helots* their freedom, an unheard-of move.

In 229BC Cleomenes marched north and annexed some Peloponnesian cities in the Aetolian League, intending to cement domestic reform by victories abroad. Poor people in many cities flocked to him, hoping that his reforms would be emulated. This initially helped him in his war with the Achaean League. But after winning two minor victories over the Achaeans, Cleomenes returned home to pursue his revolution. He executed four conservative *ephors* and abolished their ancient office. With Sparta's army now hugely increased, he

Below: This scene of martial readiness comes from the Vix Crater, *which was made in c.500BC when Sparta was in its austere prime – an age some reformist kings wished to revive.*

seemed poised to conquer the whole Peloponnese. In despair, the Achaean League's leader Aratus called in the Macedonians, his bitter enemies, and their combined forces defeated Cleomenes at Sellasia in 222BC. He fled into exile in Egypt, where he committed suicide, while Sparta itself fell to invaders for the first time in its history. But the problems – principally the growing gap between rich and poor – remained, and not just in Sparta.

THE LAST SPARTAN KING

In 207BC Nabis, who was of royal blood, took the throne probably after murdering the young king Pelops. He at once re-enacted Cleomenes' reforms but in an even more drastic manner. Forming a private bodyguard of freed *helots* and mercenaries, he seized land from the rich to pay for the restoration of the common meals so important to Spartan life. Adroitly allying with Rome in the Second Macedonian War (200–197BC), he survived until a disgruntled Aetolian officer assassinated him in 192BC. Sparta was then forcibly enrolled in the Achaean League. When Rome destroyed the

Achaeans in 146BC, Sparta became technically free under Rome's protection, but it was now a museum city. The emperor Augustus restored its port and it long continued its strange customs to entertain Roman tourists.

Above: Young Spartans Exercising, *painted by Edgar Degas in 1860. Among Sparta's unique features had been the way girls also exercised nude, shocking other Greeks. This way of life was in decay by the 3rd century* BC, *ruining Spartan strength. But some Spartan customs were long maintained to amuse Roman tourists.*

UTOPIAN REVOLUTIONS

Growing social and economic problems in many cities fused with Stoic teachings of the universal brotherhood of men to create an explosive mixture in the 2nd century BC. The founder of Stoicism, Zeno of Citium (333–262BC), had outlined in his *Republic* (now lost) revolutionary proposals for the just society, but his ideas had remained just ideas: Stoic philosophers in Athens were no firebrands. However, Zeno's ideas were elaborated by later thinkers such as Iambulus. He wrote *c.*200BC about a mythical Island of the Sun, a communistic utopia (though that word had not been invented) where all men were equal and worshipped the Sun-god. Slave risings, common at the time and always put down with great brutality, arose out of pure misery.

Especially appealing, therefore, was the utopian state that Aristonicus, the illegitimate half-brother of Eumenes II, the last king of Pergamum, attempted to inaugurate.

Eumenes had left his kingdom, which included Ionia, to the Romans in 133BC, but most Ionian cities had no wish to become subjects of Rome. When Aristonicus proclaimed his utopian City of the Sun at Pergamum, freeing slaves, many Greeks, including the Stoic philosopher Blossius of Cumae, joined him. Their army defeated a consular Roman army. It took Rome three years' hard fighting before its legions could crush the Greek utopians. Rome's revenge, typically bloody, marked the final end of Greek political experimentation.

THE WESTERN GREEKS
320–211 BC

In the 4th century BC Taranto (Taras) was the wealthiest city in Greek Italy, thriving on its trade, wool production and the purple dye obtained from molluscs in its lagoons. The philosopher Archytas guided its mixed democracy while also remaining on good terms with Dionysius I, tyrant of Syracuse. But after Archytas' death c.340BC, the Tarentines felt threatened by Italian hill tribes, despite having a large fleet. They summoned Alexander of Epirus, brother-in-law of the great Alexander, to help them, but he was murdered in 330BC. Then a far more formidable enemy emerged: Rome, expanding into southern Italy, founded Venosa, a military colony, only 144km/90 miles north of Taranto while extending the Via Appia, its first great military road, south-east towards Brindisi. The Tarentines grew alarmed.

Above: Hieron II's long reign in Syracuse (269–215BC) saw unprecedented peace and prosperity. The altar he erected was the longest ever built at c.200m/650ft.

Below: Pyrrhus, king of Epirus (319–272BC), fought as a mercenary general for the Italian Greeks against Rome 280–275BC. His initial victories proved so costly they became known as 'Pyrrhic'.

TARANTO AND ROME AT WAR

In 282BC the Greek city of Thurii, Taranto's rival across the Tarantine Gulf, appealed to Rome for help against Lucanian raiders. The Romans reacted by sending a fleet into the Gulf. This broke an earlier agreement with Taranto, which in reprisal sank some Roman ships and then mocked Rome's ambassadors for speaking bad Greek.

War followed in 280BC. Taranto called in King Pyrrhus I of Epirus, the best professional general of the time, to help it. His skilled army, with its elephants and *phalanxes*, was expected to crush the amateur Romans. Pyrrhus indeed won two

THE SACKING OF SYRACUSE

After Hieron's death in 215BC, his grandson Hieronymus sided with Carthage after Hannibal's seemingly crushing defeat of the Romans at Cannae. This catastrophic mistake led to his murder amid chaos. The Romans rallied and sent Marcellus, one of their best generals, to subdue Syracuse. Despite Archimedes' brilliant weapons (they included catapults and, reportedly, burning mirrors), the Romans finally took the city by surprise assault in 212BC.

Marcellus had ordered Archimedes' life be spared. But in the general slaughter the great scientist was killed by a Roman soldier, who, speaking no Greek, did not recognize him. Archimedes' fate epitomizes his city's, for Syracuse was ruinously sacked by the Romans, with Marcellus carrying off the finest artworks himself. Incorporated into the province of Sicily, of which it became the capital, Syracuse never regained its old importance or vigour.

major victories, marching almost up to Rome's walls. But the Romans fought doggedly on, learning to counter the elephants and replacing their own losses. After one victory, Pyrrhus exclaimed that he could not afford another such – hence 'pyrrhic (unaffordable) victory'. But, seeing the Romans methodically pitching camp each night, he admitted that his enemy was "not barbarian".

After Pyrrhus withdrew from Italy in 275BC, the Romans advanced south and Taranto had to accept a Roman alliance. By 272BC all of Magna Graecia ('greater Greece', Italy's Greek cities) was in Roman hands.

THE STRUGGLE FOR SICILY

The order that Timoleon had brought to Sicily, especially Syracuse, did not long survive his death in 334BC. In 317BC Agathocles overthrew Syracuse's government with Carthaginian backing. He made himself dictator and won support from the lower classes by terrorizing the rich. Quarrelling with Carthage, he then boldly invaded Africa itself in 310BC, but had to withdraw in 307BC. But he still made himself ruler of most of Sicily, even capturing Corcrya (Corfu) and taking a royal title. After his death in 289BC his successor, Hicetas, was defeated by the Carthaginians and deposed. In the ensuing chaos, Carthage looked set to conquer the whole island until King Pyrrhus briefly intervened.

After Pyrrhus left Sicily, Hieron, one of his officers, seized power in Syracuse. He was acclaimed king as Hieron II after defeating rampaging Italian mercenaries. Hieron ruled Syracuse remarkably well for 54 years (269–215BC). He revived some of its past glories, helped by his wife Philistis' descent from Dionysius I. Shrewdly switching to support Rome in the First Punic War (264–241BC), Hieron gained most of eastern Sicily as his kingdom. He adorned Syracuse with public buildings, including the world's biggest altar (200 x 22m/650 x 74ft), and employed Archimedes, the great scientist, to fortify it. Hieron also built the largest warship yet seen, the 5,000 tonner *Alexandria*. His tax system, the Lex Hieronica modelled on the Ptolemys', took one tenth of crops grown in the kingdom – a relatively light tax, which the Romans copied. Syracusan prosperity is revealed in the fine private house recently unearthed.

The rest of Sicily was not so fortunate, being long fought over between Carthage and Rome – Acragas (Agrigento), then, Sicily's second richest city, was twice

Right: The Colosseum in Rome, the city whose fast-rising power increasingly dominated Greek politics.

sacked and once burnt. Sicily became after 241BC Rome's first *provincia* (province), ruthlessly exploited for its wheat farms. The slave gangs who worked these huge farms revolted en masse in 135–132 and 104–100BC. Meanwhile, Greek urban life decayed.

Above: Taranto (Taras) was the richest Greek city in Italy, with a fine double harbour and a thriving purple dying industry. Yet, despite hiring the finest general Pyrrhus, it fell to Rome in 272BC.

THE SHADOW OF ROME
220–188BC

In 217BC a peace conference was held at Naupactus (Lepanto) to try to end Greece's constant wars. Agelaus of Naupactus, welcoming the delegates, pointed to the titanic struggle between Rome and Carthage then racking Italy. Now, he said, was the time when Greeks must join together like men wading through a torrent, "for if the cloud now rising in the west should spread to Greece, I fear we shall be begging the gods to give us back the chance to call even our quarrels our own."

PHILIP VERSUS ROME

His prophetic words were applauded by the delegates. However, Philip V of Macedonia, attending the conference, then made a fatal error. After Hannibal's great victory at Cannae in 216BC he, like most people, thought that Rome was doomed and so allied himself with Hannibal. He had his reasons – Roman power had been pushing down the Illyrian (Dalmatian) coast toward Macedonia. But Philip failed to realize that Rome had vast reserves of manpower and was now also the strongest *naval* power in the Mediterranean since creating its navy in the First Punic War (264–241BC). Macedonia, in contrast, had let its once fine navy decay. (On the only occasion on which a Macedonian fleet entered the Adriatic, trying to carry reinforcements to Hannibal, it fled as soon as it saw Roman ships.)

The First Macedonian War (215–205BC) was rather a non-event. Rome was too busy with events in the western Mediterranean to send large forces to Greece. The treaty of 205BC simply restored the *status quo ante*. But Rome was now increasingly interested in Greek affairs, while some Greeks thought they could call on this new power to help them in their disputes with each other.

In 200BC Rhodes and Pergamum, both of which distrusted the Seleucids and Macedonians, told the Romans that the two kings had made a secret plan agreeing to divide up the Ptolemaic Empire. They had probably not, but that year Antiochus III defeated the Egyptians at Panion, annexing southern Syria and Palestine. Meanwhile Philip seemed to be menacing Rhodes and Pergamum. Convinced, Rome declared war, sending its now battle-hardened legions east. With Aetolian cavalry to help, Philip's army was routed at Cynoscephalae in 197BC, and his power restricted to Macedonia. In particular, he gave up the 'chains of Greece', the forts that had held Greece captive. He was, however, left on the throne of Macedonia

'FREEDOM' FOR GREECE

Greece, declared the victorious Roman general Flaminius to a congress at Corinth, would now be free. Roman troops would

Above: Flaminius, the Roman general who defeated Macedonia at Cynoscephalae in 197BC and then promised Greeks 'freedom' at Corinth.

Below: A relief from the Temple of Neptune of c.100BC in Rome reveals Greece's growing cultural impact on the Romans.

be withdrawn shortly. The delighted Greeks applauded so loudly that "birds dropped from the air stunned", and they hailed Flaminius as a god, the first (not the last) Roman so honoured. But what Flaminius meant was that Greek cities could enjoy much the same limited autonomy as cities in Italy did as 'clients' of Rome, not that they would be totally free. From this misunderstanding came much later grief. But Rhodes, Pergamum and the Achaeans at the time happily accepted the peace, with only the Aetolians disgruntled at gaining nothing. In 194BC Roman troops duly left Greece.

THE FIRST SYRIAN WAR

By 200BC Antiochus III the Great seemed on top of the world. He had restored Seleucid suzerainty over the east, at least in theory; beaten the Egyptians and finally won southern Syria, long his dynasty's ambition; and pushed Pergamum back, regaining control over western Asia Minor to the Aegean. He seemed to the suspicious Romans to be about to recreate Alexander's empire. Worse, he welcomed Hannibal, Rome's arch-enemy now in exile, at his court. Antiochus even sent troops across the Hellespont, rejecting Roman protests.

In 192BC the Aetolian League invited Antiochus to intervene in Greece proper. After some hesitation and diplomatic manoeuvres, Antiochus despatched 10,000 men – enough to annoy the Romans, but not enough to impress potential Greek allies. So began what Rome called the First Syrian War. Defeated on land by the Romans at Thermopylae in 191BC (the Aetolians gave no real help), Antiochus' fleet was defeated at Myonessus after a hard battle by a combined Roman and Rhodian fleet. Finally at Magnesia in Asia Minor in 190BC, Antiochus' grand army, 70,000 strong with chariots, elephants and *cataphracts* (armoured cavalry), was routed. Scipio Africanus, who had defeated Hannibal, masterminded the Roman victory, but Pergamum's cavalry

won the day, defeating the Seleucid phalanx, which fought to the bitter end.

Pergamum had its reward two years later in the Treaty of Apamea, which gave it almost all Asia Minor west of the Taurus Mountains. Rhodes made useful gains too. The Seleucid Empire now ended at Cilicia, and it had to pay Rome 15,000 talents in reparations – a cripplingly vast sum, though payment was phased.

Above: Monument to the Battle of Cannae in which Rome suffered seemingly total defeat by Hannibal in 216BC. This led Syracuse and Macedonia to ally with Carthage.

Left: Hannibal, Rome's greatest enemy, was welcomed at court by Antiochus III, a move by the Seleucid king that roused Rome's enmity.

GREECE MADE CAPTIVE
188–146BC

Above: Perseus, last king of Macedonia, was utterly defeated by the Romans at Pydna in 168BC. His kingdom was divided into four client states before being annexed by Rome in 144BC.

Below: The circular Temple of Hercules Victor (once called the Temple of Vesta) in Rome is truly Hellenic in style. It was probably built in c.120BC by Greek craftsmen.

If Rome's policy toward the Greeks in the next decades often seemed brutal and hypocritical (promising freedom at one moment, crushing any sign of independence at the next), this reflected Rome's own ambivalence. Beyond ensuring that no power could challenge Roman hegemony, the Senate was divided. A few senators had little wish for new entanglements in Greek affairs, but other, more ambitious, Roman politicians wanted plunder and glory in the Greek east. There they could depose kings, be hailed as gods and amass unprecedented wealth. Further, Greeks themselves began coming to Rome with their quarrels, making Rome their judge.

Not all Greeks accepted this. Democrats in the cities now looked to Macedonia against Rome – many cities in Greece and Asia were still democracies, although Rome favoured oligarchies. The monarchs also had their discontents – and strengths. Although the Seleucids had lost

their western lands, their empire still stretched east to Persis and south to Egypt's frontier. Macedonia likewise retained its old recruiting grounds. Ptolemaic Egypt, however, was in terminal decay although hugely rich, clinging desperately to its Roman alliance. Only Pergamum, now booming, willingly toed the Roman line.

THIRD MACEDONIAN WAR
In 179BC Perseus succeeded his father Philip V in Macedonia. Although he renewed the treaty with Rome, he forged marriage ties with both the Seleucids and the king of Bithynia (north-west Asia Minor), while overhauling the army. This alarmed Eumenes II of Pergamum, who persuaded Rome that Perseus posed a new threat. The result was the Third Macedonian War (171–168BC) in which Rome mobilized huge forces. Perseus' crushing defeat at Pydna in 168BC, despite the success of his phalanx charge, marked the end of Macedonia. Perseus was taken in chains to Rome, where he died in prison; Macedonia was split into four republics. When these quarrelled, Rome finally made Macedonia a province in 146BC.

> **THE SACK OF CORINTH**
> By 148BC the Achaeans had had enough. Filled with patriotic fervour, they declared war, hoping that the just-started Third Punic War would preoccupy Rome. It did not, and an army under Mummius was despatched. In 146BC the Romans razed Corinth, Greece's richest city, to the ground, Mummius choosing the best artworks for himself from among the ruins. Achaea became a Roman Greek province, its League dissolved.

ANTIOCHUS' AMBITIONS

In 175BC Antiochus IV seized the Seleucid throne. He was ambitious and talented, if also eccentric – he 'stood for election' like a Roman magistrate, probably mocking the new superpower's constitution if also bewildering his subjects. But he had the old Seleucid ambitions toward Egypt. In 169BC he invaded Egypt, overrunning most of it. Rome sent an envoy, Caius Popilius, who traced a circle in the sand around Antiochus and told him not to step beyond it until he agreed to withdraw. Antiochus, not wishing to challenge Rome, withdrew.

On his way home to Syria, he stopped in Jerusalem, where the Hellenizing faction of the priestly state of Judaea (one of many priestly states in his kingdom) appealed for help. Not realizing that Jews were somehow *different* from his other Semitic subjects, Antiochus despoiled the Temple, installed a Syrian garrison and erected a temple to Olympian Zeus on the site. This was probably just part of his general Hellenizing programme. But the furious revolt that broke out, led by Judas Maccabeus the High Priest, finally drove the Seleucids from Judaea for good. (Rome supported the Maccabees). However, Antiochus' attention was focused on the growing Parthian threat to the east. With his death in 164BC, the great days of the Seleucids were over, although the kingdom survived for another century.

DELOS: SLAVE ISLAND

The Romans, thinking that Rhodes had not supported them wholeheartedly against Perseus, deprived it of the tiny island of Delos in 167BC, which became a free port. It also rapidly became the greatest slave market yet seen, reputedly able to handle 10,000 slaves a day.

Right: The flow of skilled Greek captives into Rome gave rich Romans ample domestic slave labour, such as this maid. From a fresco at Herculaneum.

The slaves were mostly Greek or Hellenized people, victims of Rome's new aggressiveness. In 167BC the whole population of Epirus was enslaved, 150,000 of them glutting the slave markets. Direct taxation was abolished that year in Rome – not a coincidence.

CLASHES BETWEEN ROME AND THE ACHAEANS

In 166BC Rome took 1,000 mainly democratic hostages from the Achaean League, although the League had supported Rome. Among them was Polybius the historian. Polybius had Philopoemon, head of the Achaean League, wonder: "Should we work with our masters and not object, so that soon we get even harsher orders, or should we oppose them as far as we can, so... we can check their impulses?" The Achaeans did both after Philopoemon's death in 182BC, clashing with Rome when it demanded they relinquish not only Sparta, which was reasonable, but also Argos and Corinth both of which had been League cities for generations.

Above: If Rome conquered Greece politically, Greece conquered Rome culturally. Socrates was among the philosophers educated Romans came to revere.

CHAOS IN THE AEGEAN
150–80BC

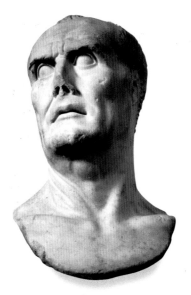

Above: Sulla, the brutal if highly effective Roman general who sacked many Greek cities in 86BC.

Below: The Temple of Poseidon at Sunium outside Athens. It escaped the fate of the city itself, which was sacked by the Roman Sulla for supporting Mithradates, king of Pontus.

The Romans had mixed, sometimes ignoble, motives behind their actions toward the Greeks – greed and paranoid suspicion must have been the most obvious to the Greeks, if not ones that the Romans would have recognized. However, Rome can hardly have foreseen the disastrous consequences of its actions.

LARGE-SCALE PIRACY
By making Delos a 'super-port', soon very popular with Italian merchants, it wrecked the basis of Rhodes' wealth. This undermined Rhodes' fleet, which had kept down piracy. Piracy now revived on a new and massive scale. (Athens, to which Delos was theoretically restored, now lacked the strength or will to reassert its old thalassocracy, sea-power.)

By 100BC pirates were raiding right across the Mediterranean from strongholds in Crete, Lycia and Cilicia, where they lived beyond any law. Slaving was one of their main activities, and they attacked Roman as well as Greek shipping. At one stage pirates captured the young Julius Caesar. Waiting for his ransom to be paid, Caesar told his captors that he would catch them and have them crucified. They laughed; he kept his word. But although the pirates attacked far up the coasts of Italy, at one point even capturing Roman magistrates off the coast of Latium, the Romans did almost nothing to check this threat until the *Lex Gabinia* of 67BC.

TAX REFORMS AND CORRUPTION
Worse still for Greece, the concessions made by Gaius Gracchus to Roman *publicani* (tax-farmers) in 122BC to win support for his radical reforms at home led to a new venality in Roman provincial administration. The tax rates levied on provinces such as Macedonia and Achaea may have been no higher than earlier, but the *publicani* extorted vastly higher taxes from the hapless provincials for their own profits. It was a disastrous way of raising revenue.

By the 1st century BC Roman government had grown detested as the proconsuls (governors) themselves became openly corrupt, knowing they faced no real danger of prosecution back in Rome. As Cicero, the great Roman writer, said: "No words can say how deeply we are hated by foreigners because of the foul behaviour of the men we have sent out recently to govern them."

Cicero's successful prosecution of Verres, an infamously corrupt governor of Sicily who had plundered the island, was as rare as his own probity while governing Cilicia.

THE RISE OF MITHRADATES
Greek colonies had long been dotted around the Black Sea, but after Alexander's reign Greek culture began to penetrate inland also. Pontus, a fertile, well-wooded region on the south coast with abundant mineral deposits, was

ruled by kings of Iranian descent who became increasingly, if superficially, Hellenized. One of these kings, Pharnaces I (220–185BC), extended his power around much of the Black Sea.

Mithradates V Pontus (c.150–120BC) was the most powerful king in Asia Minor after Pergamum's end. His son Mithradates VI Eupator (120–63BC) became one of Rome's greatest adversaries and the last, rather unlikely, champion of Greek freedom. Mithradates V started by extending his power around almost the whole Black Sea, annexing the half-Hellenized kingdom of the Cimmerian (Crimean) Bosphorus in 108BC. This kingdom, which controlled Greece's vital grain supply, was threatened by Scythian tribesmen and so welcomed Mithradates' protection. He had less success with kingdoms in the Anatolian interior such as Cappadocia, but Tigranes of Armenia became his son-in-law, guarding his eastern flank. Meanwhile he built up a formidable army under a Greek general, Archelaus.

THE SACK OF ATHENS

This army was first tested in 88BC, when, reacting to an attack by his neighbour Bithynia, Mithradates swiftly overran western Asia Minor. His proclamation of liberation from the loathed *publicani* delighted the Greeks. When he crossed over to Greece itself, even long-neutral Athens rose in his support. A massacre of 80,000 Roman and Italian *publicani* and other businessmen forced Rome into a vigorous response. Sulla marched east with 100,000 men to defeat Mithradates at Chaeronaea and Orchomenus.

Athens, which he besieged through the winter of 87–86BC, surrendered too late: Sulla's army sacked the city, even removing columns from the Temple of Olympian Zeus to Rome. Other Greek cities were similarly devastated and had to pay Rome a massive indemnity. This was collected by *publicani*, who also charged interest of 50 per cent on unpaid taxes. This crippled Greece for decades.

Problems with his rivals in the Popularis party in Rome soon claimed Sulla's attention, however, and he agreed to a peace on a return to the *status quo ante* in 85BC. Mithradates surrendered all his gains and retreated to his Black Sea empire. But his strength had only been tried, not exhausted.

Above: The Agora of the Italians at Delos. After being made a free port by Rome in 166BC, Delos boomed, attracting many Italian businessmen.

Below: Mithradates VI, king of Pontus, Rome's last formidable enemy in the Hellenistic East.

THE POWER OF THE DYNASTS
84–42 BC

Above: While the Romans fought each other, Parthia became Persia's successor east of the Euphrates under kings such as Mithradates I. He was still happy to be titled Philhellene, however.

From the sack of Athens in 86–85 BC on, the fortunes of the Greek world were inextricably linked with those of Rome's feuding dynasts – heads of the city's noble families whose ambitions tore the Republic and its empire apart.

Sulla returned to Rome to become dictator, purge his enemies in a bloodbath, reorder the constitution on deeply reactionary lines and then suddenly, to general astonishment, retire in 80 BC. While his seemingly iron-cast settlement in Rome soon started unravelling, he had also left much unfinished business in the Greek world and a thoroughly unstable situation in Asia. Egypt, although theoretically still independent, now leaned heavily on Roman support. Many Romans became tempted by the idea of annexing this, the Mediterranean's richest kingdom, but, being unable to agree on how to do so, left it shakily independent for the time being. A brief war with Mithradates in 84–83 BC came to little, but the king's strength remained undiminished.

HOSTILITIES AND MITHRADATES

In 73 BC Rome faced its most serious slave revolt ever when Spartacus raised a force soon amounting to 150,000 men in Campania. The revolt took two years and a major military campaign to suppress. Meanwhile, Mithradates, alarmed at how Rome was handling its new acquisition of neighbouring Bithynia, bequeathed to it in 74 BC, renewed hostilities. He invaded Bithynia, again threatening Rome's position in Asia. Lucullus, an associate of Sulla, was sent east with a large army to subdue him but faced problems with a mutinous army and Mithradates' skilful tactics. Gradually, however, he exhausted Mithradates by the usual Roman attributes – tenacity and willingness to endure high casualties. Mithradates finally had to seek refuge with his son-in-law in Armenia. (Tigranes had extended his power south to create a large kingdom.) Before Lucullus could kill either of them, he was recalled in 66 BC. His command passed to a far more dashing general.

POMPEY THE GREAT

Pompey was (relatively) young and handsome and had a fine military record when the *lex Gabinia* gave him wide powers to deal with the pirates. Swiftly raising a combined land and sea force of 100,000 men, he rooted out the pirates – more by bribes and threats than military action – in only three months.

In 66 BC the triumphant general was given Lucullus' command by an impatient Roman people. Over the next four years Pompey earned the title 'the Great' (which he had assumed already) by a statesmanlike mixture of diplomacy and force. Forcing Mithradates out of Pontus – to which he had returned – he drove him to his last resort: a fortress in the Crimea. There Mithradates committed

Left: Julius Caesar, charming, charismatic and unscrupulous, emerged victorious from Rome's first round of civil wars. His affair with Cleopatra VII probably produced a son and further tied Egypt to Rome.

suicide in 63BC – by the sword, after failing to poison himself. He had reputedly made himself immune to all poisons by taking a daily antidote.

With Mithradates dead, Pompey rearranged the east at leisure. Tigranes' empire was abolished but he was left in Armenia, which became a client state of Rome. So did a string of small kingdoms from the Caucasus down to the Red Sea. Pompey, capturing Jerusalem, entered the Holy of Holies in the Temple, gravely if inadvertently offending the Jews. Judaea also became a client state. The rump of the once great Seleucid Empire became the Roman province of Syria, ultimately the new centre of Roman power in the east. Pompey's settlement was brilliant: it almost doubled Rome's revenues and lasted in essence more than 100 years. Pompey returned to Rome in 62BC to celebrate another triumph.

GREECE THE BATTLEFIELD

In 49BC the first in a new round of civil wars broke out in Italy when Caesar, returning from conquering Gaul, 'crossed the Rubicon' into Italy proper without disbanding his army. (His many enemies had prevented him from standing for consul *in absentia*, and to return to Rome as an ordinary civilian would have been suicidally risky.) Greece found itself the hapless battlefield as Roman dynasts battled for supremacy. Pompey retreated to Greece where, in 48BC, he was defeated at the Battle of Pharsalus in Thessaly, being killed soon after when he landed in Egypt. Caesar, in hot pursuit, had a different encounter, with the young Cleopatra VII, co-monarch with her brother Ptolemy XIII. She had an affair with Caesar and probably a son, Caesarion. Suppressing an uprising, Caesar made her sole ruler.

Right: Pompey entering the Temple in Jerusalem. This unwittingly sacriligious act angered Jewish priests, some of whom were killed by Roman soliders when they rioted. From a medieval manuscript by Jean Fouquet.

Right: Pompey was Caesar's chief rival in the struggle for supremacy in Rome.

After Caesar's assassination in 44BC, another round of Roman civil wars racked the Greek world. The conspirators, or 'liberators' as they styled themselves, Brutus and Cassius, crossed to Greece to raise fresh armies. To pay for them, Cassius exacted yet more money from the exhausted Greek cities. Brutus and Cassius were defeated by Mark Antony at the double Battle of Philippi in November 42BC. The Roman Empire was then provisionally divided, Antony taking control of the east while Octavius Caesar, adopted son of Julius, took control of the west.

CLEOPATRA AND ANTONY
50–30 BC

Above: Cleopatra, as this bust suggests, was not stunningly beautiful, but she was witty, charming and very wealthy – qualities Antony appreciated.

Below: The meeting of Antony, victorious Roman overlord of the East, and Cleopatra, last Hellenistic queen of Egypt, was one of unparalleled splendour, here envisaged by the great 18th-century painter Tiepolo.

By 50 BC only Egypt, fabulously rich, remained independent of Rome. The Ptolemies relied on Roman support against external aggressors, but internally their rule was insecure. Alexandria was increasingly turbulent, while in Egypt proper the over-taxed *fellahin* and priesthood no longer supported the dynasty. Intermarriage between sister and brother, an Egyptian custom the Ptolemies adopted, may explain the feebleness of later male rulers. Their queens, in contrast, proved ruthless and dynamic. Before the dynasty's end, one great queen tried to restore Ptolemaic glory.

Cleopatra VII was born in 69 BC, daughter of Ptolemy XII. From 51 BC she was co-ruler with her younger brother and husband Ptolemy XIII. When Pompey, fleeing from Julius Caesar, landed in late 48 BC, Ptolemy XIII's agents executed him and presented his severed head to Caesar, expecting him to be delighted. He was

not – Caesar prided himself on his clemency. He was, however, won over by the youthful charms of Cleopatra, smuggled into his chambers in a carpet. Or so legend goes.

CLEOPATRA AND CAESAR

Cleopatra was not, if contemporary portraits are honest, especially beautiful, but she was intelligent, charming and witty. She was ambitious, too, wanting to restore the Ptolemies' former empire. Her affair with Caesar, a womanizer of immense charm, probably produced a son, Caesarion. Caesar supported her against her brother, but the Alexandrian mob took against the Romans. Vicious street fighting led to part of the Library being burnt and almost to Caesar's and Cleopatra's death. They were saved by Jewish guards, which made Caesar pro-Jewish. Cleopatra duly became sole monarch. In spring 47 BC, with order restored, Caesar hastened away. Cleopatra later followed him to Rome, there to witness his assassination in 44 BC and the recurrence of Roman civil war. Returning to Egypt, she watched and waited on developments.

THE GREAT LOVERS

Mark Antony had been Caesar's trusted lieutenant, giving his funeral oration. Now he had to accept young Octavian, Caesar's great-nephew and adopted son, as an equal partner in the Second Triumvirate (pact) in 43 BC. But he was regarded as the better soldier and, by many Romans, as a better man. He also got on well with Greeks.

After his victory at Philippi in 42 BC, Antony wintered in Athens, debating and dining, before sailing east to be hailed as the god Dionysus by the Greeks of Asia. But although divine, he was still short of money. When he summoned Cleopatra

Right: Cleopatra (as painted by Cabanel, a 19th-century French artist) was not really Egyptian by culture or descent. But Roman propaganda portrayed her as a decadent oriental femme fatale, bewitching Antony.

to meet him at Tarsus in Cilicia, he wanted her wealth, not her body. But Cleopatra made a spectacular entry. "The barge she sat in, like a burnished throne/Burned upon the water. The poop was beaten gold:/Purple the sails and so perfumèd that/The Winds were love-sick with them" as Shakespeare, following Plutarch, later put it. Antony fell in love with her – and she probably with him – and they sailed to Alexandria for a winter of amorous luxury. They founded a club, the 'Inimitable Lives', revelling through the night, and cruised up the Nile. When he bet her that she could not eat a dinner worth a million sesterces, she dissolved a vast pearl in wine and drank it. Antony's role as Dionysus was apt, for the wine-god was the Ptolemies' patron deity. Cleopatra herself often appeared as the goddess Isis.

Meanwhile, Octavian faced major problems – revolts in central Italy, attacks on Rome's grain supplies – that forced him to ask Antony for help. This was given. In 36BC Antony's grand attack on Parthia proved a disaster, although he made Armenia a client state in 34BC. At the 'Donations of Alexandria' that year, Antony sat enthroned beside Cleopatra as she was hailed as Queen of Kings. He gave provinces from Rome's empire to their two children and hailed Caesarion, Caesar's son, as King of Kings. Cleopatra's ambitions seemed fulfilled.

DECLINE AND FALL

All this was a marvellous propaganda gift to Octavian. His poets depicted Antony as bewitched by an oriental *femme fatale*. Even so, when war was declared in 32BC, a third of the Senate went east to join Antony, whose forces were still large. But Antony alienated Roman supporters by letting Cleopatra join him in Greece, and desertions began. The final battle at Actium in 31BC was an anticlimax, Antony and Cleopatra fled south to Alexandria for a last winter of love. Octavian followed the next year. After another defeat, Antony tried to kill himself. Dying, he was reunited with Cleopatra, who had retreated to her mausoleum. There she cheated Octavian of a triumph by poisoning herself with asps. If Antony had won, Egypt would have remained independent for longer and the Greek cities might have enjoyed more independence, but the Roman Empire would not have been radically different.

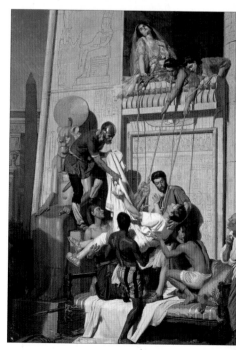

Right: Antony, dying from stabbing himself, was finally reunited in death with Cleopatra in the mausoleum to which she retreated.

AUGUSTUS AND THE PAX ROMANA 27BC–AD14

Above: The Corinth Canal, the construction of which was started under the philhellenic emperor Nero in AD66.

Below: The theatre at Taormina in Sicily, where a Roman superstructure sits on a Greek base, exemplifies how Greek and Roman cultures intermingled. Taormina was Greek in origin while Sicily itself only became fully Hellenized under Roman rule.

The death of Cleopatra VII marked the end of the Hellenistic age. The whole Greek world west of the Euphrates now lay under Roman control, directly or indirectly. Much of it had been ravaged by Rome's own civil wars: the grandfather of Plutarch the historian had been forced to carry sacks of grain on his back up mountains for Antony's army during the Actium campaign in 31BC; Corinth was a gutted ruin; Athens, though still a revered intellectual centre, was exhausted; so were the once brilliant cities of Ionia.

AUGUSTUS' RULE

Augustus, as Octavius was soon titled, had triumphed as leader of upright Romans against what he had depicted as a decadent Hellenistic world. The Greeks perhaps at first expected little from this Roman emperor (from Latin *imperator*, commander), but they were agreeably surprised. Augustus spent two years in the East, re-establishing it along lines laid out by Antony and Pompey. Herod the Great was confirmed in his Judaean kingdom, as were rulers of petty Hellenistic states fringing Rome's eastern provinces.

Roman frontier provinces such as Syria were governed by legates sent out by the emperor, often commanding legions stationed there. Egypt alone was treated differently, becoming the private fief of Augustus governed by an equestrian (knight) not a senator. This reflected imperial nervousness about giving power to a potential rival from the Senate. The first governor was Gaius Gallus, chosen because, as a poet, he might appeal to Alexandrians. (Unfortunately power went to his head and he was forced to commit suicide.) Augustus wisely refused to attack Parthia. Although he extended Rome's northern frontiers, to the Mediterranean world itself he brought peace, the long-lasting Pax Romana.

LOCAL GOVERNMENT

Most provinces in the Greek world, such as Achaea, Macedonia and Asia (western Anatolia), were governed by proconsuls appointed by the Senate if overseen by the emperor. The letters between the emperor Trajan and Pliny the Younger *c.*AD110 show just how close this supervision could be. Such governors had few troops, for much of the Roman Empire long remained lightly guarded and lightly governed. Most of the governing was done by local citizens themselves.

The empire has been called a 'confederation of cities', although the population remained mainly rural. But the local aristocracies – Rome never favoured democracies even when a republic – administered their own cities, competing to build ever grander temples, baths and theatres. (A few cities such as Tarsus had Roman rights, meaning that citizens such as St Paul were Roman citizens.) Rome's light-touch imperialism stemmed from its own lack of bureaucracy, reflecting Roman preferences. Alexandria was ruled directly, but it had long lost its council.

PROSPERITY REGAINED

Linking the cities of the newly stabilized, extended empire was a remarkable network of roads, ultimately covering 80,000km/50,000 miles. These encouraged trade, but sea routes remained far more important. Here the suppression of piracy, started by Pompey and maintained by Augustus and his successors, was crucially important.

The resulting boom saw Corinth, refounded under Augustus, become a wealthy port again. Old Ionian cities such as Miletus, Ephesus and Smyrna became unprecedentedly rich, with populations passing the 100,000 marks, as did Hellenistic cities such as Alexandria and Antioch. Athens enjoyed renewed if modest prosperity, exporting its fine Pentelic marble – and craftsmen – while educating young Roman aristocrats. Augustus built a grand new agora and *odeion* (roofed theatre) in Athens, and a small temple for the cult of Rome and Augustus on the Acropolis, stressing Roman power at the heart of Greece.

TAX REFORMS

Also of crucial importance were changes in the tax collection. Caesar had wanted to abolish the rapacious and loathed *publicani* (tax-farmers) outright, aware of their ruinous effects. The more cautious

Below: The Temple of Hera at Acragas in Sicily, whose partial recovery under the Pax Romana was typical of many Greek cities.

Augustus gradually replaced them with appointed officials whom he could trust. Taxation for most provinces was relatively small. The sales tax, for example, was only 1 per cent, and customs dues were 5 per cent. Where *publicani* survived or were introduced, their rapacity could engender revolts, as in Britain in AD61 and Judaea in AD66.

TWO CENTURIES OF PEACE

At the end of his life in AD14 the emperor Augustus was moved by a demonstration. The passengers and crew of a ship just arrived from Alexandria, greatest of Hellenistic cities, put on garlands and burnt incense to him, saying that they owed their lives and liberty to sail the seas to him.

This peaceful prosperity continued for another two centuries. The walls of most cities not actually on the frontiers, even of Rome itself, were allowed to decay in a period that was, by historical standards, phenomenally peaceful. No wonder that most Greeks were happy to honour Augustus and his successors as divine – honours that wiser emperors did not boast of in Rome itself.

Above: The Temple of Hadrian at Ephesus, one of many Ionian cities that attained its greatest prosperity in the 2nd century AD under the long Pax Romana. Hadrian was a famously philhellenic emperor.

Below: A cameo of Augustus, the first Roman emperor (27BC–AD14). Augustus admired the High Classicism of Periclean Athens.

GRAECO-ROMAN SYNTHESIS
CICERO TO HADRIAN, 80BC–AD138

Above: Bust of Cicero, the Roman orator, writer and politician who summarized and translated into Latin many works of Greek philosophy, ensuring their survival.

Below: The Maison Carrée in Nîmes, a Roman colony in southern France. The temple, built in Augustus' reign, embodies Graeco-Roman synthesis, for its columns are classically Greek but its plan is wholly Roman.

In 80BC Cicero, an intensely ambitious young Roman politician, arrived in Athens to study philosophy. He was among the first in a stream of Romans who, over the next 400 years, would go to Greece to study philosophy and rhetoric. Cicero's stay had a huge impact on philosophy over the next 1,500 years in Western Europe. While his prime interest was politics, he turned to writing philosophy full-time when forced into (temporary) retirement by Caesar's ascendancy in the 40s BC. In a few years he summarized in Latin much of Greek thought, especially Stoicism, in *De Republica* and *De Finibus* ('Concerning the Highest Ends'). In his books, which survive intact unlike most ancient literature, he established Latin equivalents for basic Greek philosophical terms such as morality, quality and happiness.

Cicero's achievement in translating and synthesizing Greek thought typifies the growing Graeco-Roman fusion.

After 200BC Greek culture had flooded into Rome in the form of looted artworks and thousands of slaves, the latter often better educated than their masters. They became secretaries, librarians, doctors and tutors. While Roman nobles tended to regard Greeks politically as irresponsible, deceitful and even decadent, many admired Greek culture almost uncritically for a time.

The temple of Hercules Victor in Rome, built *c.*120BC as a perfect circle with slender marble columns, is almost wholly Greek in form. Equally Greek are the wall paintings – surviving best in Pompeii thanks to Vesuvius – probably made by Greek artists working for Roman masters. By Cicero's time, educated Romans were fluent in Greek. A century later Quintillian, the Roman grammarian who taught the sons of emperors, suggested that boys should learn Greek before they learned Latin, so essential was it to their education.

NERO'S INFLUENCE
"Greece made captive captured her conqueror and introduced the arts into rough Latium," wrote Horace, one of the emperor Augustus' chosen poets. If this Roman cultural inferiority was fading by the early 1st century AD – mainly thanks to Horace and other great Latin poets such as Virgil – Greece was still seen as the exemplar, even by some emperors.

In AD54 the 17-year-old Nero, the last of Augustus' descendants, became emperor. With genuine artistic interests if not talents, he patronized artists and architects – especially those building and adorning his vast new imperial palaces – and composed plays. Seneca, Nero's tutor and first minister, wrote philosophy and tragedies, which, if not publicly staged at the time, survived to influence later playwrights such as

Right: Admetus and Alcestis Listening to the Oracle, *a fresco from the 'House of the Tragic Poet' at Pompeii,, reveals how familiar Romans became with Greek myths and how popular Greek styles were in Italy in the 1st century* AD. *This work copies a Hellenistic original.*

Shakespeare. But Nero performed in public himself – something thought shameful for a noble Roman – at first in Naples, a still Greek city. He also tried to introduce Greek athletic games without success. When Nero entered the Olympic Games, he won *all* the prizes, the first and last time this happened. More positively, he proclaimed 'freedom' for Greek cities and ordered the digging of the Corinth Canal, although his engineers stopped when they hit bedrock. Nero's reign ended in civil war in AD68, however, and there was a brief Roman reaction under his successors.

THE PHILHELLENIC EMPEROR

In AD128 the emperor Hadrian dedicated the Pantheon, temple to all the gods, in Rome. This most famous and best preserved of Roman temples exemplifies Graeco-Roman synthesis. Behind a giant portico essentially Greek in inspiration rises a majestic dome wholly Roman in conception. Hadrian, who commissioned and possibly helped to design it, was the most philhellenic of all great emperors, to the point that his enemies called him Greekling (*graeculus*).

Regarding Athens as his favourite city, he made it head of a new Panhellenic League and built an entire new quarter, besides completing the Temple of Olympian Zeus started 640 years before. He was elected archon (the office still existed), initiated into the Eleusinian Mysteries, the holiest in Greece, and wore a beard like a Greek philosopher.

Equally Greek was his passion for Antinous, a youth of royal descent and so his social equal, to be wooed not raped. Hadrian's grief at Antinous' death struck many as undignified, but in his reign (AD117–138) the Greek-speaking half of

the empire finally recovered its self-confidence and began to supply important officials. Under Hadrian too began the systematic codification of Roman laws, where Greek humanism and idealism lightened Roman pragmatism.

TWO-WAY INFLUENCE

The influence did not run all one way. The Greeks adopted some Roman architectural features, using arches and vaults more often. Gladiatorial games, that most Roman entertainment, were also introduced to the Greek world. Initial revulsion – there was a riot in Antioch at the first – evaporated as Greeks, too, developed a taste for these brutal thrills. More positive and far more significant was the emergence of a new Graeco-Roman ruling class, exemplified by men such as the orator Aelius Aristides or Dio Cassius, a Greek who became a Roman consul and historian. By AD200 a single Graeco-Roman culture had developed across the empire.

*Above: The emperor Hadrian, in whose reign (*AD117–138*) Greeks became almost equal partners with Romans. Hadrian himself was made archon of Athens, a city he loved deeply.*

GREECE REBORN:
RENAISSANCE AND RENASCENCES

Above: Desiderius Erasmus (1466–1536), the pioneering Renaissance scholar who learned Greek to translate the Bible, so unwittingly paving the way for the Reformation.

Below: The stadium at Olympia, site of the ancient Olympic Games last held in AD393.

Linked to Rome, ancient Greece declined with it. The last Olympic Games was held in AD393; five years later invading Visigoths ravaged the peninsula, looting the temples. Finally, in AD529 the Academy in Athens was closed on the (east Roman) emperor Justinian's orders. Early Christianity, though Greek-speaking, was almost as hostile to Hellenism as the barbarians were. By AD600 ancient Greece was dead. All knowledge of Greek was lost in Western Europe. *"Graceum est: non legitur"* ("it is Greek, not read") medieval monks wrote besides passages in Greek. Only translations of Aristotle from the Muslim world, which retained some Greek knowledge, revived interest in that philosopher in the 13th century.

THE REVIVAL OF HELLENISM
The ghost of Greece, however, lived on. In 1438 the Council of Florence tried to reconcile differences between the Eastern and Western Churches. It had small success, but among the Eastern bishops was Bessarion, a scholar who stayed in Italy, befriending other Greek fugitives after Constantinople fell to the Turks in 1453. They brought with them manuscripts – principally by Plato, Greece's greatest

philosopher – which Bessarion collected. In Renaissance Florence, Cosimo de' Medici founded a Platonist Academy in 1462 to study Greek and philosophy. Soon Plato's birthday was being celebrated, and Socrates was being hailed as a pagan saint, by cardinals and princes as well as scholars.

ART AND THE SCRIPTURES
The Renaissance engendered a Platonic desire (as *eros* best translates) for spiritual truth incarnate in physical beauty. Newly discovered Roman copies of Greek statues inspired Renaissance artists. Botticelli's *Birth of Venus* illustrates Greek myth in romantic Neoplatonist mode, while Michelangelo created art sublimely Platonist in aspiration. If this artistic and intellectual rebirth hardly affected politics – democracy was unthinkable in Renaissance Europe – it resurrected classical art in the Western world.

> ### THE ENEMIES OF DEMOCRACY
> For many scholars Socrates has been seen as a martyr to intellectual freedom, put to death by the rudely ignorant mob. But this veneration can at times lead to ambivalence about democracy itself. Socrates exists for us mainly in the pages of Plato, and Plato was no friend of democracy. In the 20th century, as totalitarian tyrannies on the right and left flourished, the political philosopher Karl Popper attacked Plato as one of the great enemies of the 'open society', inspiring Fascism *and* Communism. Popper's attack (in *The Open Society and its Enemies* 1945) coloured more than one generation's views, although it has since been criticized. The questions and dilemmas first raised by the Greeks remain alive to trouble or inspire us to this day.

A novel use of Greek was for studying the Scriptures, originally written in Greek. Desiderius Erasmus (1466–1536) was amazed to find the Vulgate (Latin Bible) riddled with errors. His translations and biting commentaries caused a furore, paving the way for the Reformation. Erasmus spent years in England teaching Greek at Cambridge University, which became a centre of the New Learning. Queen Elizabeth I herself learned Greek. By 1600 knowing Greek was essential for any self-respecting scholar. But Hellenism's full impact had yet to be felt.

THE SHOCK OF THE OLD

In the late 18th century, travellers returned from Greece with news of a radically simple yet powerful architecture. Finds at Pompeii, that time capsule of Graeco-Roman art buried by Vesuvius, were already leading the arts toward a purer Neoclassical style. But the brutally gigantic Doric columns seen in classical Greek temples amazed Europe and America. Confronted for the first time with true classical Greek architecture, architects reinvented their own art. The British Museum in London, the Brandenburg Gate in Berlin and much of Edinburgh shows how Greek temples could be lovingly recreated in the most unlikely places.

The late 18th century was the age of revolution in America and France. While the American Founding Fathers looked mainly to Republican Rome for models, the Achaean League's federalism also inspired them. Full democracy, not thought practical in America in the 1780s, was embraced in revolutionary France ten years later. Some French Revolutionaries, following the philosopher Jean-Jacques Rousseau's primitivist ideas, looked to Sparta as an ideal state. But the full (male) franchise, fleetingly achieved by the First French Republic for the first time for 2,000 years, was inspired by democratic Athens. Not by coincidence, fashions of the time echoed those of Greece and Rome in architecture, furniture and women's clothes.

Literature reflected the new 'Hellenomania'. Poets in England such as Keats and especially Shelley, who wrote dramatic poems such as *Prometheus Unbound* modelled on Aeschylus, supported radical democratic politics. Shelley's friend Lord Byron gave his life in the cause of resurrecting Greek liberty. Politically, the Greek precedent became ever more inspiring as democracy spread in the 19th and early 20th centuries. Abraham Lincoln deliberately modelled his Gettysburg speech on Pericles' funeral oration. Later generations still feel the lure of Greece, the true birthplace of democracy.

Above: The Pantheon in Rome, Greek in its name (meaning 'for all the gods') and fusing Greek and Roman ideals, is the finest ancient classical building extant. It was an inspiration to Renaissance artists and architects, especially to Raphael (1483–1520), who is buried inside it.

Right: The Laocoön, the remarkable Hellenistic statue whose rediscovery in Rome in 1506 proved a crucial inspiration for Michelangelo, the greatest Renaissance sculptor.

INDEX